Why Did God Save Me?

Why Did God Save Me?

Proof of my Spiritual DNA

Dr. Simone M. Duplessis, ThD

Founder and Pastor, Ecclesia of Christ Fellowship Center

XULON PRESS

Xulon Press
2301 Lucien Way #415
Maitland, FL 32751
407.339.4217
www.xulonpress.com

© 2020 by Dr. Simone M. Duplessis, Th.D.

All rights reserved solely by the author. The author guarantees all contents are original and do not infringe upon the legal rights of any other person or work. No part of this book may be reproduced in any form without the permission of the author. The views expressed in this book are not necessarily those of the publisher.

Unless otherwise indicated, Scripture quotations taken from the King James Version (KJV)–*public domain*.

Printed in the United States of America.

ISBN-13: 978-1-6312-9421-1

Dedication

I dedicate this book to my heavenly Father, the head of my life. I thank Him for electing me, for without Him none of this would be.

In loving memory of my mother, the late Velma Picquet Duplessis, who taught me to smile, even when the world doesn't smile back at you!

To my ninety-year-old father, Antione Duplessis, Sr., who instilled good values in me and my eight siblings: "Work will not kill you; it will only strengthen your character and conduct."

In loving memory of my godmother and first-grade teacher, the late Barbara Ann Nolan-Richard, who repetitiously said, "Always seek higher education and independence, and never be afraid to travel the world."

To my only son, Deacon James T. Bridges, Jr., whom I love so dearly, I thank you for making it easy to raise you because of your humble and kind spirit.

To my beloved Ecclesia of Christ Fellowship Center the Elect Lady and her children, whom God has entrusted to me.

Table of Contents

Dedication v

Introduction ix

Chapter 1: Saved to Serve God 1

Chapter 2: Saved to Serve Many 5

Chapter 3: Saved for God's Plan 13

Chapter 4: Saved to Live out My Purpose 49

Chapter 5: Saved for Eternity 55

About the Author 65

Bibliography 67

Summary 69

Introduction

We all are victims waiting to be rescue from something or someone. We became victims back in the "Garden of Eden, when Adam and Eve" (Gen. 2–3 KJV) were influenced by the serpent to go against God. Through a gift called "free will," they made the wrong choice by choosing what the serpent said over what God commanded them to do. We became victims and not victors when they went against God.

Even today, this remains true: every time we go against God, we as the children of God become victims, because we've received the "spiritual DNA" of victors. Since then, there is this need to be rescued. Believe me when I say, humanity longs deep in their hearts to be rescued from hate to love, darkness to light, lies to truth, void to substance, curses to blessings, selfishness to selflessness, and ungodliness to godliness, each and every day.

A fireman is the one we see running into a building, blazing with fire! Meanwhile, everyone else is running out of the same building, blazing with fire! Isn't it funny that after the fireman rescues the victims, for some reason the victims feel they owe the fireman for saving their lives? But God did the same by saving you many times over and over, and what do you owe Him! Why do you think God saved you?

The paramedics received a 911 call, from an office where you worked. After arriving the paramedics noticed you were on the floor, nonresponsive. They began to work on you with chest compressions but still you were nonresponsive. They've worked longer and even harder, but still you were nonresponsive. It was announced over the radio the symptoms supported signs of a heart attack.

The paramedics take you to the nearest hospital emergency room. You were told, according to the heart monitor, you flatlined in route to the hospital. You believed the paramedics saved your life! Therefore, you feel you owe the paramedics for saving your life. But God did the same by saving you many times over and over, and to what do you owe him? Why do you think God saved you?

The domestic engineer (DE) walks into your hotel room where you hung the sign on the door said, PLEASE DO NOT DISTURB, but somehow, the door hanger was removed by accident, so you think! As the DE enters the room, it appears to her you've overdosed on drugs. She dialed 911 for the operator to contact the paramedics to get you to the hospital in time to save you. You will even go back to find the DE to thank him/her for saving your life. But you will not seek God. Why wouldn't you seek God, to see why He saved you? God said, "If you seek me with your whole-heart you will find me" (Jer. 29:13 KJV).

I'll attest to seeking God with my entire heart; it was after surviving the storms of my life, I realized I should be dead, I could be dead, and I would be dead if it wasn't for God, who came and rescued me, and I began to "search out God's word with my whole heart" (v. 13). I wanted to know, "Why did God save me?" See I felt like you; I owe my rescuer, but I didn't know my rescuer, not as a personal friend but a mutual friend, not directly but, indirectly. God is definitely a personal and relational God!

Chapter 1

• • • • •

Saved to Serve God!

"God and suffering according to, Peter Kreeft there are two categories of suffering: Moral evils which are done by humanity, and natural disasters for instance, earthquakes, hurricanes, chronic illnesses, sarcoma/cancer, pestilences, plagues and the Novel Coronavirus (COVID-19 virus) which are done by nature" (Kreeft, 2014). I can honestly say that through suffering I became closer to God, but not at first. Instead, I was angry! I was introduced to God by my mother, who in turn was introduced to God by her mother, and her mother's father, who was a deacon in the eighty-nine-year-old church of the town in which we lived, which after the following hurricanes did not and could not destroy the eighty-nine-year-old church building. This church was left leaning for Hurricane "Betsy" (1965), and the entire community gathered together and reconstructed it because it was left standing with only the framework for Hurricane Katrina (2005), and they rebuilt again! "This is how God reveals Himself to humanity, in a broad sense—it's called general revelation" (Jibben, 2016). Here's the backdrop on the word of God in my life and how others cling to God. I lived in a rural area at the time, and you could walk to and from school. Things were different back then. Being a basketball player, I had a basketball game this particular night. I was walking, on the highway to go to the school, and I was accompanied by approximately nine other people, eight children and one adult. As we walked, a car drove by, hitting something; I remember hearing the horrific sound even now! Some things you will never ever forget as long as you live!

Well, we all kind of absquatulated out of the way of the car, but didn't know the suffering we were about to endure. Lo and behold, it was discovered when we gathered ourselves together we found one was missing. The alleged driver had dragged my schoolmate with the car a couple of feet away from us. Later, I found out my very own cousin was the alleged driver. Even today, that was a case never really legally resolved, which means some believe there was allegedly another driver involved with that accident that never came forward. Needless to say, the bereaved family went to the parent's house of the alleged driver that was incarcerated and did what a true Christian would do, even in the midst of suffering: they took upon themselves an act of forgiveness. Whether we know it or not, forgiveness is symbolic for God bringing people closer together, regardless of their suffering.

Meanwhile, I am struggling to understand why an all-knowing, all-loving, and all-powerful God would allow this manner of suffering to come upon His people. You see, I was dealing with the impact of the accident, entirely different than others. I became so angry with God; I remember being angry for about eight years. The ending of this story is twofold: I was saved at the age of eight, only because that was my family's way, custom, culture, and faith from the scriptures, which say, "Train up a child in the way they should go . . ." (Prov. 22:6 KJV). Little did I know my classmate was searching for God the Holy Spirit. When I would invite her to church—yes that same church mentioned above—she would come and go to the church with me. Her comment was, "You know, I feel His presence here, but not anywhere else."

It took me some years, to come to understand what she was saying to me. I asked God, why did he save me? He finally answered me, and He said, "You have work to do!"

"I was angry because of the suffering, but it was suffering that brought me closer to God" (Jibben, 2016). Now, I have a personal relationship with God, and He's drawing me closer, day by day. Apostle Paul wrote to the church of Philippi, "Being confident of this very thing, that He which hath begun a good work in you will perform it until the day of Jesus Christ" (1:6 KJV). I've read and heard the historical biblical scriptures of Job, whom God called "My servant." God asked, Satan, "Have you tested my servant Job? No doubt God knew where Job was in his heart, as it related to their relationship. But for some reason Satan wanted to try Job anyhow. Satan mentioned these words to God: "When you allow his worldly possessions to be taken away, will he still love you?" God said, "Let's put my servant to the test, but one thing for sure; you can remove everything except, the hedge of divine protection." Satan said to God, 'Okay!' Satan began to strip Job of all his worldly possessions. But still, Job loved and trusted the Lord" (Job 1–3 KJV)!

Just remember, when the next storm comes in your life, God's will for you is to be like a tree. God willed you to be rooted, and grounded, so you will bend, but you will not break. This is the strengthening of your character and conduct for your role, which is a significant part of your purpose. God will cause or allow the necessary events to take place in your life to put you in a position to be rescue, redeem, and restore back in right relationship with Him. Knowing the historical biblical passage of Job, I believe a good, loving, and all-powerful God allows suffering and evil within His creation to humble us or for us to remain humble, to guide us back/close to Him, to constantly remind us He's our Creator; we need Him in our everyday walk.

In this case, one might say, well, Job was humble or it's for Job to remain humble, or it's for others around him to draw closer to God, to see the glory of God through the evil works and sufferings done by Satan to humanity. This is how we come to know God, directly or indirectly: directly if you have a personal relationship with Him, and indirectly if you know Him traditionally or through someone else, like a mutual friend, "in the power of his resurrection and the fellowship of his sufferings, becoming like him in his death" (Phil 3:10 KJV). Suffering joins people closer to Christ and his sufferings, especially in persecution (Matt. 5:11–12 KJV). Who wants a friend when the minute the wind blows, the rain falls, and the water rises your friend is gone and left you all alone. Jesus said, I'll be a friend who sticks closer than a brother. A true friend will go with you to it, in it, and through it! Jesus promised, "I'll be with you always even until the end" (Matt. 28:20 KJV). Ironically, God and suffering are in the same sentence because in life, you'll not have one without the other. God will let you know He's there for your time of peace and time of war, joy and pain, weakness and strength.

I was saved by God through faith in the blood of Jesus Christ and compelled by the Holy Spirit that dwelt in me. Therefore, as I come to know more about God, it draws me closer to God each and every day through the suffering of my natural man to the transformation of the supernatural man. I've come to realize I was saved by the love of God to take upon the mind of Christ and led by the Holy Spirit, in order to serve God!

Chapter 2

● ● ● ● ●

Saved to Serve Many!

Do you remember Joseph from the eleventh of the twelve tribes of Israel or the twelve sons of a wealthy nomad who went by the name Jacob (Israel) and Joseph's mother was Jacob's second wife, whose name Rachel? All parents has a favorite child; the only way a parent doesn't have a favorite child is if the child is the only one. This child is understood to be the favorite.

Well, the book of Genesis 37–50 tells us that Joseph was Jacob's favorite child; he was so loved by his father. Jacob loved Joseph because God had blessed him with this child in his old age. You see, we don't seek out the understanding of why something is the way it is, but we take what "we think we know" and go our own way. The Bible says, "There's a way that seems right to every man but, it's not . . ." (Prov. 14:12 KJV). If we pray about the things we do not understand, God will bring the truth to the light. The love Jacob had for Joseph was more between him and God than him and Joseph. Joseph was symbolic for the love God had for Jacob. It's no doubt Jacob (Israel) had prayed to God for this child, and God knows what else was attached to his prayer. But how can the things of God be understood by the carnal mind versus "the mind of Christ" (Phil. 2:5 KJV)? This is what you really should notice. Joseph was a type of Christ. How? He was the beloved son of Israel, from prisoner to prince. Jesus was denied by Peter, betrayed for thirty pieces of silver by Judas and loved ones and those closest to Him, from judgment hall to judgement hall, like a criminal or prisoner, but yet a Prince. Joseph experienced the same circumstances, situations, and issues in his arena of life.

God saved Joseph because he had a plan for his life. When God saved you from the pits of hell, know that you're saved by God's saving grace to save many.

Be aware to accomplish the plans that God has for you; you will need to start with the authority that is the word of God and the anointing—now, that cost. Salvation is free—that's Jesus's part, but I promise you the anointing will cost—that's your part! The anointing will cost you your entire heart. God said, to love Him with your whole heart, so you must have discipline to be a disciple. To know how to follow prior to leading, one must be fit for service. You must be ready to offer yourself up for the sacrifices of praise, spiritual gifts, talents, time and service, obeisance, humbleness, meekness, compassion, passion, selflessness, godliness, and a truth spirit. The only way to worship is in the truth and before the truth. Believe me when I say, there will be times—yes plural—when you stand for right and you'll find yourself standing all alone. Know this: Jesus is with you. There are times folks will go against you—even plot against you like the chief priests and the entire Sanhedrin council. They sought after Jesus but, not in the way you think. They were looking for any kind of information to prove their corroboration against Jesus. They wanted him dead and didn't even have the authority to crucify him. It's just like you and I, folks seeking to tear you down before they build you up. This is another element to the peak of the prophetic structure. John wrote, Jesus said, "Moreover, if you raise me up I'll compel the masses unto myself" (John 12:32 KJV). The Jews could only stone Him to death. This means we must know the enemy and know what the enemy can and cannot do. It's amazing how the enemy would like to do copious evil towards you. Nevertheless, the enemy does not have the authority over you. Here it is God's saving grace: we will die when God says we will die, and we will live how God says we will live, and we will endure if God says we will endure. It's not a man within humanity can change the plan God has for you. Not even you! The enemy wants to back you up. No, he doesn't have your back; he'll force you into a corner with no space, and when your back is against the wall, he will offer you all he has, but what you don't know is that he doesn't have anything, and by this time he's seduced you to sign his temporary contract. Don't let the enemy corner you. You will find if the enemy has a house he's just housesitting; if he has a car, it's on lease. Basically he will tell you whatever you want to hear. Just like back in the Garden of Eden, there are no new tricks.

If you find yourself talking to the enemy, you should already have the living word hidden in your heart, the one you're going to allow to flow from your heart and out of your mouth. When I am backed into a corner, this is what I say from time to time, I find myself making this statement: please don't make me choose between you and God. You'll lose every time! Be aware of those folks who will enter into your arena of life and expect you to put God on the back burner for them. What you haven't realize yet is they put God on the back burner a long time ago. God has an intelligent spirit and infinite wisdom. We are to reflect God by resembling Him. Therefore make wise choices.

When we don't choose wisely, we leave doors open for the enemy to come in, and the enemy will sit with deceit, talk with jealousy, and even laugh with persecution. He doesn't stop; he continues with lies, lies of character assassination, if not worse, physical death.

We all know that love is an action word; in representation of that love Jacob gives Joseph a coat of many colors, which reminded his other sons constantly of his love for the favored child.

Remember earlier I noted in chapter one that with God and suffering, according to, Peter Kreeft, there are two categories of suffering: moral evils, which are done by humanity and natural disasters—for instances, earthquakes, hurricanes, chronic illnesses, sarcoma/cancer, pestilences, plagues, and the novel coronavirus-COVID-19, which are done by nature" (Kreeft, 2014).

Well, Joseph's life teaches us many lessons, for instance, a form of suffering by the hands of God's pinnacle of creation. Yes, the biblical facts show that his very own deceitful, jealous, and persecuting siblings sold Joseph into slavery.

But, later Joseph rose to continue in life and not stop in death. Many preachers called this particular life experience "The Pit to the Palace." You see, what man meant for bad, God will turn around for your good and His great work. Again, "sufferings come to strengthen you" (Rom. 8:5–8 KJV). Here's where God show His sovereignty. God does what He pleases. God will utilize your enemies in His plan.

Even though Joseph's siblings sold him into slavery, what they didn't know was God had a plan for Joseph to arrive in Egypt, which proves they too were being utilized without an idea of the plan of God. Evidently they paid for Joseph to get to Egypt by the Ishmaelite's caravan (cousins). Joseph didn't even pay for his "ride to rise" in Egypt. This is what God has whispered to me time after time: "God will provide provision for the purpose." This is exactly what He did for Joseph. What He's done for others, He'll do for you! What He's done once he can do again!

If you feel you're victims of the people closest to you, just hold on a little while longer. God will step in and turn it around for your good and his great work! You see, in Egypt, Joseph rose to become Pharaoh's most powerful man, his second in command. Joseph went from victim to victor only by the hands of God and not humanity. It's not until we recognize "who's we are in Christ" that we will ever understand the plan that God has in store for the "good to those who love God, who are the called according to His purpose" (Rom. 8:28 KJV).

The word of God speaks about giving thanks in both bad and good. I believe in life experiences, we are to give thanks for good and bad relationships. It is there in that place of life that we find out our strengths and weaknesses. I used to ask this question all the time: "Why do you give your all and others do not pour into you what you pour into them?"

God answered one day and said, "The strong must bear the infirmities of the weak . . ." (Rom. 15:1 KJV). Well, at that time I was looking around for the strong, and I can truly say today, it's true! We seek things from others that are not there and may not ever manifest. Therefore, we're seeking something in relationships with others that God has "already placed inside of us" (Gen. 1:11 KJV). One's heart will not surrender love if there's no love in one's heart. One's heart will not surrender kindness if there's no kindness in one's heart. One's heart will not surrender gentleness if there's no gentleness in one's heart. I once heard a quote, "Hurt people hurt people" (Bowen, 2016). The seed of hurt can only produce pain, and the seed of sorrow can only produce tears, and the seed of sadness can only produce depression. Nevertheless, the seed of joy produces laughter and strength. According to Nehemiah, the devil don't want you joyful because after "joy comes your strength" (10:8 KJV)!

I remembered I was in a relationship, and evidently the other person was hurt deeply by someone else. Of course, I read the book mentioned above after this bad relationship. Well, the relationship lasted only a very short time because of the actions the other person was trying to induce into the atmosphere of the relationship.

You see, when others do you wrong—the first time, for instance, attempting to introduce you to abuse, be it verbal, physical, or psychological—it's their fault. If it happens the second time, and the time after that, it's your fault. Because you've made a moral, ethical choice to stay and be treated as such, because you must know that one level of abuse will lead to another level of abuse. Believe me when I say, there is another level.

The fact about hurt people will hurt others is so true. Be aware when you're dealing with and/or around hurt individuals. I remembered an old folks' saying, "If a person loves you, they'll do anything for you, and if they don't love you, they'll do anything to you." What power lies in the propositional phrase of a 3–2 letter word, for you verses to you? I believe it to be true, because I know of a husband asking his wife to clean her handgun, and after cleaning the wife's handgun, the husband left his wife's handgun hammer half-cocked, and the chamber was fully loaded with the purse straps twisted around the hammer of the handgun, set to go off. When the wife would have awakened for church the next morning, the unexpected was supposed to happen. There's proof of the mother-in-law and the man on the phone discussing the wife's assess' and life insurance policy. They began to tell people how unstable the wife was acting. It is here you will find what others meant for bad, God meant for your good and his great work! As much as the wife went to church, she didn't wake up on time to make the church service this particular morning. When she didn't go to church, she was able to find her handgun a couple of days later after a heated argument with the husband.

It's something in each and every one of us, immediately following the rescue mission there's always the innate ability that kicks in and has this urge to know, why did God save me from the hands and plans of the devil? She began to reflect back on the facts about Joseph in her relationship: "But as for you, ye thought evil against me; but God meant it unto good, to bring to pass, as it is this day, to save much people alive" (Gen. 50:20 KJV). We all must come to understand, if God does not approve your relationship, the relationship will not work out. I am constantly reminded God is an agent of free will and therefore will not force you, but He will cause you to do what it takes to get you back on track. I know that lesson all too well!

Remember you're saved to serve many. For instance, a car dealership custom designs every car, which is unique to itself. The sedan has four doors for its role, the SUV has a certain height for its role, and the sport car is low to the ground and with high speed for its role. But, "the role is significant to its purpose" (Warren, 2002). The purpose of the sedan is designed to carry a family, the purpose of the SUV is to go through water and over the neutral ground, and the purpose of the sports car is designed for performance. Here's the question: when looking back at your role, can you see what God has custom designed you for and how it aligns to your purpose in life? Are you custom designed for a family (sedan), custom designed for helping others (SUV), and/or single at heart with speed (sports car)? It looks strange trying to put a family of eight into a two-seat sports car. This is what our lives looks like every time we match up with folks God didn't approve of. After all, God's the Creator of us all, and He knows how He custom designed each and every one of us for our purpose.

If you're reading this book please pray prior to accepting and/or taking a mate or spouse and/or surrounding yourself with others you call friends, and ask God for guidance. Just because there was a proposal didn't mean God sent it. God wasn't the only one listening to your prayers, especially if you said them out loud. What God has for you to do is bigger than you and your role because "your role is not your purpose but, a significant part of your purpose and you're uniquely designed for the outcome" (Warren, 2002).

Chapter 3

● ● ● ● ●

Saved for God's Plan!

I believe that we are made in the image of God, and we now talk to God the way the first man, Adam, talked to God, in the cool of the day, in the "Garden of Eden" (Gen. 3:8 KJV). I believe after the creation of man was the fall of man when the first man, Adam, sinned in the Garden of Eden and hid himself from God. I also believe that after the fall of man, God loved the world so much He gave His Son, Jesus the Christ, who was crucified and died on a hill called Calvary, and three days later rose from the dead, ascended into heaven, and is now sitting, sometimes standing, at the right hand of God, interceding on my behalf and the behalf of all believers. This was done in the world to heal (redeem) that broken relationship between God and humanity.

God knew prior to Adam and Eve that even if He was to tell us in words what His vision was for this world, words couldn't describe the glorious creativity of God in His holiness. I believe that's when He began to allow the heavens, moon, and stars to come forward and the beautiful diverse color flowers to grow to share His beauty with us here on earth, He prepared a place for us in the garden, He prepares for us each and every day, and rest assured He's preparing for the new world to come. He said, "Heaven is a prepared place for a prepared people" (John 14:1–7 KJV).

Let's talk about this world and the one after we depart from this place. I believe the world is natural and of the supernatural. It seems to be orderly because God created it that way. He is the living and true God of decency and in order. I believe the universe is an "open system," the reason being that the spiritual influences of divine intervention, angelic activity, and definitely the working of miracles are still in existence today. I was introduced to the "open system" long before I studied and/or understood it. It's amazing how we invest precious time by sitting and looking at movies and/or reading a book having to do with the "open system" but still, we will not believe when God show us the "open system" through divine intervention or angelic activity.

During 2017, an elderly man about the age of eighty-six, who couldn't walk at the time, was sick in one of the local hospitals on the west side of Jefferson Parish. I was accompanied by about ten church members, and we were visiting, serving the Lord's Supper to the sick. There was also a friend visiting with the elderly man, aiding the man by shaving him. Well, we began to observe the ordinance of the Lord Supper, the testimony of the elderly man, the words of encouragement, the reading of the scripture, and out of respect for the sick, the low key singing, and the prayer. Suddenly, as the prayer was going forward, the young man who had accompanied me with the other members of the church began to lose feelings in his lower extremities; he became faint, and his mother and the others had to remove him from the room. While I was praying, all this was going on literally behind my back. Afterward, the young man was rolled down stairs in a wheel chair and to the emergency room (ER). Of course, the emergency room doctor couldn't find anything wrong with the young man. After receiving the Lord's Supper, I went downstairs to seek for the young man and the others, when I asked, how do you feel, and he replied, "I feel as though I was hit by an eighteen wheeler." I in turn said, with such faith, that the elderly man upstairs would walk by Monday, which was the next day. I returned to the hospital to see if he was walking. Before I could ask, he said, "I just got back in my room. The therapist had taken me down stairs to walk." Won't He do it! I dare not boast in the presence of God. I know He's the one and only living God of this world.

I believe, "In the beginning was the Word, and the Word was with God, and the Word was God. There was nothing created without him . . ." (John 1:1-3 KJV). Don't get discouraged when God renders to you something of the supernatural that appears to be nothing in the natural, but wait a little while, and you will see the "ex nihilism factor," which means God will take nothing and create something—for instance, a church building with empty pews but in a little while, the building is too small to hold the members.

To the local churches be careful what you're filling the church pews with; I'll take souls over members any day. You do your part and allow God to do His part. This is why the word of God says, "Apollos watered, Paul planted, and I give the increase" (1 Cor. 3:6 KJV). Therefore, God validated His own part; now you must do your part. Jesus said, "I'll draw all men unto me" (John 12:32 KJV).

God loved us so much that "Jesus became flesh and dwell amongst us . . ." (John 1:1, 14 KJV). Therefore, God the Father, God the Son, and God the Holy Spirit is the Triune God. He sent His son to set an example for us, how to live here on earth as the natural man, but yet know that after death in this world, we have another home after this life as we know it. This second life consists of the supernatural world (New Jerusalem) to come. This world is future tense. But, first from dust we come and dust we shall return. "We don't know what we shall be like but, we shall be like him, in a moment in a twinkling of an eye . . ." (1 John 3:2, 1 Cor. 15:52 KJV). Now, this is for the believer because the nonbeliever has a different place to go.

Let's talk about knowledge, which is very important for the Christian journey, I believe knowledge is the ability to reason: its one's perception how they understand and interpret something or someone, data that is collected and placed in memory. It's one's consciousness and must be true and validated. "The fear of the Lord is the beginning of knowledge . . ." (Prov. 1:7 KJV). I believe if one asks God for knowledge he will bless you with a gift of knowledge.

Now, let's combine knowledge with ethics derived from the Bible in the library of law as it applies to the book of Exodus: "Thou shall not kill" (3:20 KJV). Ethics are accepted and have become my moral standards to live by. For this reason human life is more precious than "things." Things can be replaced, but not a human life. So, I am highly influenced by the good behavior, integrity, custom, character, biblical scriptures, or writings of the Bible that enforce good behavior versus bad behavior. Ethics are what we do not do, even though we have the knowledge to implement them. One may have knowledge of the right thing to do and still not apply it, but to have the knowledge and to implement it is ethics in my book, God-conscientiousness versus a natural conscientiousness, if there is such a thing.

This brings me back to, why did God save me? I was saved for God's plan, but I must understand who God is in order for me to understand the plan God has for me. Therefore, I believe I was designed to worship and to praise God. Worship is in the writings of Saint John (4:24 KJV): "God is a Spirit. They that worship Him must worship Him, in spirit and in truth." Praise because, I was delivered by the love of God, the blood of his Son, Jesus the Christ, and the communion of the Holy Ghost to show forth the praises to the Creator who created Adam on the sixth day of the Creation, in which Adam represents all mankind. Because the Creator sought after me and called me out, now I must diligently seek after Him and call upon Him. "But you are hand pick by God, you're of royalty in the priesthood, a nation that bears holiness, God's special possession, that you may declare the praises of Him who called you out of darkness into His wonderful light" (1 Pet. 2:9 KJV). I must work the works of Him who sent me while it is day; the night is coming when no one can work. "Man does not and will not defined me, my works through Jesus Christ defines me" (John 10:32 KJV). If God didn't save me, I would have stopped on this journey a long time ago. Listening to others' opinion about who God called, people are putting God in a box, saying who God called and who he didn't, and practicing more tradition than rightly divining the word of God to benefit their own inadequacies. God sent a warning of this in the books of Jeremiah and Ezekiel. Once again, man has limited God, basically telling others who God called to what office in His house. I was taught the church is God's by ownership, the pastor's by stewardship, and the congregants' by membership. If, this is true the Captain (God) gets to say who steers the ship. Our sin nature will always get us in trouble, which is what happened back in the garden. God commanded Adam to keep and maintain the garden. Once Adam was allowed to come in the garden, he wanted to own the garden. If I remember correctly, stewardship involves relationship, meaning how you care and manage for something, but not ownership. I believe this is how he got evicted from the Garden of Eden. When we act like Adam, we began to look like Adam, and Adam reflected the devil more than he reflected God. The reflection of the devil looks like this when you allow your flesh to manifest the following fruit: "adultery, fornication, uncleanness, lasciviousness, Idolatry, witchcraft, hatred, variance, emulations, wrath, strife, seditions, heresies, envying, murders, drunkenness, reveling, and lies" (Gal. 5:19–21 KJV).

    Earlier, I've mentioned about others' opinions, but it was more than opinions; it was a protest, disapproval, disagreement, opposition, challenges, and demurral, to say the least. I had attended secular colleges and universities, as well as, one seminary in particular at this time. I was installed as the Elect Lady of God to the office of pastoral care. I was also serving my country. But it's very heartbreaking to have folks around you who take on negative actions, expressions, and feelings towards you as to what they believe God called you to do—or should I say, didn't called you to do. When I say folks, I am speaking about folks near and far, inside and outside, in other words. I am basically describing some things Jesus went through with the near and far, the inside and outside. That discrimination doesn't always come from abroad; it can come as close as family, it can come as near as friends, seminarians, preachers, pastors, and associations. In the word of God it is said, a prophet is not received in his close circle of life. It's complicated living peacefully with those especially of the faith because you're constantly fighting, over your interpretation of the scripture versus someone else's. Here's one I've witnessed often. A male pastor walks into the room and he's immediately acknowledged as such: pastor and/or reverend. When they get to you, the female pastor, they want to strip you down from the pastoral office, and if they could strip you of your education, they would do that also. Here's one for example. I remember witnessing a female who had a bad stammer when she had to call another female by title/name who just so happened to be a pastor. I've even heard a person literally choke and the clearing of the throat on the words Pastor Duplessis when addressing me. Sometimes based upon what he or she believes they'll even call me Sister Duplessis. I've witnessed it enough to know the arrogance and sometime the ignorance of it to know just what's being done. I thought this was taken care of back on August 6, 1965, during the African American women's suffrage movement. Men and women struggle with the pastoral office God called me to more than I do. But for some reason I believe it's more women struggling than men. For example, Ms. Mary

Saved For God's Plan!

goes to see the doctor for the first time, and she has a new primary care doctor. When he walks in the room. Ms. Mary says to the man who walked into the room, Good morning Doctor Benny. Don't know if he's a doctor or not. I have all the credentials I need and more but, when will it be enough? They will not give you the equal respect not even servants of God.

A couple of years ago, the Gatekeepers' Baptist Association was in session. This is an association that I am a member of .I am also the director of the youth department. I was the guest speaker on this particular day. I remember telling the congregants, if you want to know how someone feel towards you or what level of respect they have for you, listen closely for the title of respect or how they address you. For instance, if a mother didn't raise her little boy, most likely he was reared by the grandmother, so if the grandmother raised the child, the child will call the grandmother mother and will call the mother by her first name. This shows the level of respect within the mother and son relationship. The same is for the pastor and his flock: pay attention. When the flock says reverend or elder but not pastor, most likely you've been installed as the pastor of that church but, not of that member. I am a "baby boomer." when my mother was living, let me attempt to call her by her first name, and I would have probably preceded her in death. I don't know what's wrong with God calling a woman, especially when the calling is relational and yet personal. I pray for a change through divine intervention for those that struggle with such things in this day and age.

I remembered November 10, 2006. It was a Friday night. It was the night of my ordination ceremony. According to protocol, it's the church that pays for the ordination ceremony for the previous preachers that went through the same ceremony as I did; I passed the catechism, which consisted of a board of seven counselors (six men and one woman). The ordination ceremony program consisted of the moderator, speaker, hymnologist, bibliologist, ordination certification/documents, all fees totaling $500.00 for that one night. After, meeting all the criteria that pertain to the ordination, having the church to pay a total sum of $500.00 dollars fee for my ordination was out of the question. After the program was over, I remember feeling as if God had me in His bosom, and I began to hear Him clearer than before. I felt as if God was pleased with me for the first time in my life. From a spiritual perspective all of my life accomplishments and achievements, nothing came close to what I felt the night of the ordination. But God was getting me ready to embrace the world right in the church. Then, lo and behold, my pastor at the time came over to me while everybody was congratulating me. In the midst of it all pastor says, "The church secretary said, 'the church will not write a check for her ordination because the church association does not believe in ordaining women.'" I am talking about discrimination in the faith, among the brethren—and yes, in church leadership. Even though pastor told me the church association would not ordain me, if I got another association to place me understudy and ordain me, he would support me. Up to this day I appreciate my pastor for the support.

Do you know how it feels to have a calling from God, obtained degrees by educating one self, have been mentored by another spirit-filled pastor and evangelist, passing your catechism after studying long and hard, only to be told on your ordination night by the church pastor that the church secretary will not be writing a check to Association "X" in the amount of $500.00 because the church members and the church association don't believe God called a woman to pastor? To all female pastors the "called of God," I encourage you to do what God called you to do, the way He said to do it, and stay humble to God and kind to God's people. I am a witness; He'll show up just for you just like He showed up for me, again.

Once again God show up just for me! God provided for me in this season to be on active duty, which allowed me sufficient financial support, and a Christ-like mind for stewardship, led by the Spirit to have had the $500.00 on me the same night. Nevertheless, I was able to pay $500.00 to Association "X" the fees that were owed. You see, what man has for your bad, God plans for your good to give you an expected end. Saved once again for the plan of God!

No man has the right to say who God called to what office and who He didn't. For those of you who know what I am speaking on behalf of the struggle within yourself, it's enough to process the fact that God called you and then, to struggle with your very own family; you know it's all good until you announced God called you to the ministry. Nowadays, it's as if folks are ashamed of the Gospel of Jesus Christ, that God called you versus lifting you up in prayer.

I remember in the Bible, Jesus was healing the sick, and the disciples were gathered around. Meanwhile, Jesus's family (mother and siblings) approached the area, standing at a distance. The disciple said, to Jesus, "Your mother and siblings are here." Jesus replied, by pointing to the disciples, "They that do the work of my father whom sent me is my family" (Matt. 12:46–50 KJV). Once again, they were looking for something in others that may not manifest. Here's another event that's a mystery unto man. This is what Jesus told the disciples. I am sure man would had said, God would not allow a donkey to talk, but nevertheless, it is written, God has the power to make a donkey talk. God definitely does what He pleases and with whom He wants to accomplish it with! God is no more interested in man's opinion than the called of God should be interested in opinions.

Being enlightened and empowered by the word of God, validates the called God placed on my life for my purpose in life. Now, I must run the race in such perilous times.

I was serving beside my pastor, who at the time was courageous to allow me to work, in the office of an elder, and later promoted me as his assistant pastor. Allow me to share with you the intricate parts of my struggle while being called to the ministry.

During this particular time pastor was sick in the hospital, recovering from a heart attack. I had gone to see him to go over the church calendar. One of the events that caught my attention was a baptism coming soon. I proceeded to ask the pastor, "What are we going to do, call around to see who we can get or cancel?" Pastor said, "No! You're going to do the baptism." I had never done a baptism without my pastor. I asked, "Are you sure?" He replied, "Yes!" The pastor said, "I have no doubt in my mind if anybody can do it, you can." He supported me and assigned another minister to assist me. The minister didn't agree with me being a female taking the lead for the baptism. See struggles, while I am going down in the baptism pool being prayerful, excited about souls being saved, not that baptism has saving powers, but it is part of the salvation cycle. Instead, the minister was concerned about whether he should lead and I should follow because he's a man. I pressed my way with prayers and the strength of God, and the Spirit of the Lord came upon me. It was not by my might or by my power. That day I cried, more than the candidates!

I had another disagreement whereby one of the grandmothers of the baptism candidate refused to send the grandson to be baptized. Like I said, it's a struggle when folks don't know what thus said the Lord.

During 2013, God elected me to found/pastor my beloved Ecclesia of Christ Fellowship Center. This act of objection came later. The evangelist shared with me that a male pastor expressed to him that when he heard about resurrection Sunday morning that I had twenty-two candidates for baptism, he was going to show up at the church and stop the baptism. I'd in turn told the evangelist, there's always the First Amendment to the Constitution of the United States. The struggle is real—this was a man of faith, trying to stop me from baptizing the people of God. God is not pleased! There's a law against folks stopping worship service. Needless to say, I didn't hear anymore, and service went on just fine; all glory goes to God!

Last but not least, to testify of the goodness of the Lord, God's plan is for the pinnacle creation to worship, praise, and testify of His goodness.

I can truly live out God's plan in the world. Of course, it's not and will not be easy, but I know it's rewarding. Becoming a Christian is life changing. It changed my life in degrees of light versus darkness. I remember when I knew God as a mutual friend of my grandmother and even my mother, which was knowledge of God from a traditional standpoint. But now I can say I know Him as my direct friend, my Lord, and my Savior. I have a personal relationship with Him. It's like in the movie *The Book of Eli*—I heard God's voice, and I have answered to the call of my ecclesiastical orders. I heard the voice of God say to me "Before I formed thee, I'd woven you thread by thread, stitch by stitch, I ordained thee in your mother's womb" (Jer. 1:5 KJV). I believe I can say my quality of life is more humble, kind, peaceful, and joyful, and patience is present, in my day-to-day operation. The quality of my life and worldview is satisfying now, in spite of what I've been through.

I know Him for myself because there is not a time when He did not come to my aid in the times of trouble. I was diagnosed with sarcoma, and I could have had my left forearm amputated, but all Glory goes to God! For the last thirteen years, I am in remission.

It's nobody but God! I am so convicted that if He didn't heal me, it would be okay, because it's not like He's unable. I am like God's servant Job "though you sled me, yet will I wait until my change come" (Job KJV). That's the level of my conviction. I thank Him for my trials and tribulations, afflictions and infirmities He's allowed me to go through because this is where I get to know He's a doctor, a lawyer, Wonderful, The Mighty God, The Everlasting Father, the Prince of Peace and Counselor" (Isa. 9:6 KJV). My God has and shall supply all of my needs like no other has. If He doesn't, I still believe He's the "Maker and Supreme Ruler of heaven and earth" (Gen. 14:19; Ps. 146:6 KJV). My faith might be inadequate to someone else, but if so? I am not offended by someone else's opinion. However, this is why I have "first-faith" and not religion. Here's why because God called me out of darkness a long time ago to enter the all-inclusive— you know, the choice of the "whosoevers" of his marvelous light. What I have with God is not of this world. This world is not my home. I am a foreigner traveling through. I don't understand why people are fighting over who are citizens and who are not. That's why I can't be shaken of the love He has for me. I like how Apostle Paul wrote it: "I'll let nothing come between me and the love of God, not even when life has ended" (Rom. 8:38 KJV).

I am satisfied with Him but the question is, is He satisfied with me?

During Thanksgiving of 2018, my mother had been ill for about five years, and her heart was functioning at 10 percent, along with other medical issues. On the way to the hospital no one said a word. Then, my mother asked me, "Do we have anything else left to do?" I knew exactly what she was communicating to me, even though, it was never directly spoken. Mother's funeral arrangements were finalized nine months, prior to her death. The doctors sent her home on hospice. I would lie beside my mother in her bed and lead her in devotion. The tears begin to swell up in my eyes, but, I held the tears as tight as I held my mother, but God, revealed Himself to me and said, your mother does not need a daughter; she need a servant. This was not "the special revelation I wanted from God" (Jibben, 2015). I felt closer to God, and I realized the devotional period was stronger. Another special revelation was, as tight as I was holding my mother, I realized God was holding me. That's how I got through towards the end of her life, burial, and pending resurrection. I do miss her, and I am still trusting God. I drew closer to God by doing what He said, "comfort your mother as she transitions" (Topic 6 Overview, 2017).

I was inspired to write this poem for my mother before she died. I would like to contribute this poem to all whom have taken care of a love one on Hospice:

"From Our Cradle to Your Grave"

You held us from our cradle. Now, we must let you go to your grave.
You fed us. Now, we must feed you.
You stay up with us through the night. Now, we must stay up through the night with you.
You bathe us. Now, we must bathe you.
You clothed us. Now, we must clothe you.
You combed our hair until we grew some. Now, we combed your hair until you had none.
You are "Christ-like" because you loved us first, even when we didn't love ourselves.
You loved us from our cradle yet beyond your grave.
You held us in your bosom. Now, we must let God hold you in his.
You taught us to smile, even when the world didn't smile back.
You love us passed our faults, (oh boy, do we have faults) and you saw to our needs.
Now, we must see to your needs.
You always said, "I know my children."
You know all 9 different personalities.

Mother, it must have been love that kept you praying for us.
Mother, God has answered your prayers we are now grown women and men able to care for our children, grandchildren and great grandchildren.
When others mothers died, you stepped in and became a mother to so many others.
You even attained the title "Mother Zion," for you were the mother at the church.
We thank you for nurturing us from our cradle. Now, we must nurture you to your grave.

Until the 2nd Coming of Christ
Love, your Children   Author: Dr. Simone M. Duplessis, ThD

Meanwhile, my ninety-year-old father grieves his wife of sixty-five years at the same time teaches his nine children one last powerful lesson in life, how to wait. This poem was written after I asked my father, how did he meet mother, and this is what his story looks like in poetic form:

"I Waited"

I waited at the store, just to see you pass by,
I'd looked up the road, down the road, but you had not come by,
I waited, to take you to the movie, my sister and I.
I waited, in heart and I waited in mind I waited for some time to see what life would bring,
    waiting patiently, now we have nine.
I waited, when you asked "when will I dine?" I waited and I waited, to make Christ mine!
Good things come to those who wait, but I didn't know how much my soul would take.
I waited, for your sake and I waited for mine,

I waited, to see you in the absence of time.
I waited, to see you nigh,
Now, I wait to see you high in the sky!

Love,
Your Husband

       Author: Dr. Simone M. Duplessis, Th.D.

 He waited at the beginning and he's still waiting. Learn to "wait upon the Lord" (Ps. 27:14)!
 One of the many things I was told while serving in the armed forces was, do not talk about religion, money, and politics. But I didn't take offense because I don't have a religion. I have a faith (monotheism) that there is only one living and true God. God is an infinite, intelligent Spirit. You see, I believe faith is the art form of life, how you do something. For instance, you're the brush, your spirit is the paint, and the world is the canvas.
 It's not something we practice and hope we get it right! It's basically, a lifestyle. Your good deeds can bring a color of love to a situation of hate, a color of peace to a situation of confusion, and a color of joy to a situation of sadness.
 It is written, in the Bible "no prophet should expect to be honored in his own country" (Luke 4:24 KJV). Sometimes it's hard to be utilized by the Holy Spirit to compel our loved ones, especially those close to us. They are too familiar with who we are; they can't see past the natural man and see the supernatural.
 I was looking at the movie *The Book of Eli* (Hughes, 2010). Don't feel like the "lone ranger"; you and many others had an oversight of Eli being blind, throughout the entire movie. The more I talk to people about it, the more it's known to me they didn't know that critical fact in the movie. The majority have replied, no I didn't realize Eli was blind. Therefore, Eli, in spite of being in the midst of feeling deserted in the world along with

his afflictions and infirmities, his trials and tribulations, he still heard God's voice calling him in the midst of it all. With everything going on in the world, can we hear or recognize God's voice? If so, can we answer to the voice of God, answer to the call of God, and accomplish the mission of God?

Eli was the example of how we as Christians/Theists are supposed to walk in the world, among the nonbelievers. We as Theists should have a clearer message and understanding of "true blindness" spiritually. Apostle Paul writes in the Bible, "We walk by faith and not by sight" (2 Cor. 5:7 KJV). Eli not only read it, he believed it, hid the word in his heart, and lived by it. It's how the Christians/Theists should journey through the world seeing things the way God sees (Gen. 16:7–16; Prov. 15:3; Eccl. 12:1–14 KJV), through the "spiritual eye."

It's true, at the end of the hour, day, week, month, year, or the end of life, as we know it, that's all that matters. Did we do what God said for us to do? From time to time, I hear Christians saying, "I am satisfied with Jesus," but the true question is, is He satisfied with us? We are in a world of "building material things" that will soon pass away. Do we realize heaven and earth shall pass away, but God promised His word will stand? We must build our hope on things eternal.

Each person's belief about the origin of the universe makes an extreme difference in the individual choices in life. For instance, the Theist choice is to believe that God is the Creator of the universe, and the atheist choice is to believe God does not exist; therefore, He could not create the universe. The believer can begin to live life with an ultimate reality, whereas the nonbeliever has no reality. The believer begins to search for reasons of existence; on the other hand, the nonbeliever just exists. The believer if asked, "Why on earth am I here?" will find his Creator created him with a purpose. We were created to worship the Creator through fellowshipping with Him by walking with the

Creator, talking with the Creator, and living in the Creator's will. The nonbeliever can't ask this question because, he does not believe there is a Creator; therefore, according to him, he is not created for the plan of God or any special reason or purpose. He will walk along with no guidance; he will not have a Creator to petition for help. He lives life worshipping the creation, not the Creator—for instance, the moon, stars, sun, earth, and all the things in the earth, and of the earth; the job that is utilize to gain the house in a particular neighborhood, the luxury car, the name-brand clothes, food, and the vicious cycle of the promotion on the job.

The believer can love God. Here's the difference between knowing God, and there's no God can affect one's daily living and life in its entirety. Knowing God can aid us in giving respect to one another, and having peace with all men. When there's no God, there's no peace and definitely no order to one's life. "The unwise has said, in his most secret inner part, there is no God" (Ps. 14:1 KJV). Being a Theist, I believe nothing happens without reason. I believe that everything happens for a reason, not by chance. I believe the proof is within one of the many characteristics of God. For example, the characteristic of God in reference to:

> Teleology Argument or Teleological: God is a being of design, custom, purpose and order. Teleological argument: an argument for the existence of God which reasons that, since the universe exhibits evidence of order and design, there must be an intelligent and purposeful God who created it to function in this way (Grudem, 1994, Glossaary p. 1255).

Predestination (Rom. 8:2–30 KJV) in theology is the doctrine that all events have been willed by God, usually with reference to the eventual fate of the individual soul (Merriam-Webster Dictionary online).

I would like to bring up *enlightenment* or *reason*. After all, enlightenment back during the seventeenth and eighteenth centuries was "an intellectual movement emphasizing reason, individualism, skepticism, and science. Enlightenment thinking helped gives rise to deism, which is the belief that God exists, but does not interact supernaturally with the universe" (Kant, 1960). But of course, we as Theists don't agree with the latter.

Because one of the many promises of God, one in particular is that it is written in the book of Matthew: "And, lo, I am with you always, even unto the end of the world. Amen" (28:20 KJV). Another definition is

a philosophical movement of the 17th and 18th century, characterized by belief in the power of human reason and by innovations in political, religious, and educational doctrine. An example of Enlighten was 'The Age of Enlightenment,' a time in Europe during the 17th and 18th century considered an intellectual movement driven by reason. John Locke was an English philosopher and physician, widely regarded as one of the most influential of Enlightenment thinkers. The major figures of the Enlightenment included Beccaria, Diderot, Hume, Kant, Montesquieu, Rousseau, Adam Smith, and Voltaire. Enlightenment impact society by change government and society by using reason to improve/perfect the world and influence change globally (Kant, 1960).

They believe that human reason could solve any problem. I like the synonym of *enlightenment*: :edify, educate, inspire, nurture. Other related words to enlighten are "elevate, enrich, uplift, better, improve, regenerate, renew and transform." These are words that we as Christians read throughout the Bible, which are measures of faith, power, and force.

Basically, I truly believe with no doubt God is the Creator of the creation including the universe. Here's my reason: I see the characteristics of God, in an anthropomorphic kind of way, His arms around the universe, His footprint between the stars and the moon—or should I say His fingerprints all over the universe in and out of space and/or in the spiritual realm.

As the psalmist said, in the 145th Division of the King James Version, "Thy mighty acts, shall be praise by one generation to the next and thy wondrous works will be spoken of and here we are even this day, still talking about his wondrous works." In the book of Job, God asked, "Where were you when I laid the foundations of the earth" (38:4 KJV)? "Declare, if thou hast understanding. Job where were you when I put the stars in their sockets?"

Peaceful on the outside is not the same as peaceful on the inside or peace from within. I am peaceful as long as you don't share your beliefs with me and I won't share my beliefs with you. But, I must ask, is that true fellowship with one another? Being that our God (Theist) is a relational and personal God, I believe when we meet with one another and do not share Jesus, we are not really fellowshipping, which is a form of worshipping, or we are just meeting. Behold what about the peace from within? I heard it like this: "know God, know peace . . . no God, no peace!" "If you abide in me and I in you, ask what you will and it shall be given" (John 15:4 KJV). Because what happens when the branch does not abide in the vine? The "peace" that is mentioned above comes from no one but God! Therefore, based upon the gift of free will, I do respect the atheist and agnostic views. However, it doesn't mean I agree, but I am still concerned about their lack or voided peace from within. Remember, free will is all about the individual making the right choice, allowing the Holy Spirit to compel them into the kingdom; this is done after you work the works. If we as Christians don't respect the atheist or agnostic, how will there ever be an opportunity to minister to people with such view? I often wonder also about the void and emptiness in one's life as atheist or agnostic.

God's Plan is for the Christian life to become more and more in the likeness of Christ. Sanctification is also a part of the application of redemption which is also progressive work that's continuous throughout our earthly lives. Sanctification has a definite beginning at regeneration. Apostle Paul speaks about the "washing of regeneration and renewal in the Holy Spirit" (Titus 3:5 KJV). Once born again, the Christian can't continue to sin as a habit or a pattern of life, because the power of the Holy Spirit keeps us from yielding to a life of sin. Basically, as Christians you can't continue to love to sin. At this point, the Christian should realize who we are in Christ, sin is what I do, it's not who I am. (1) I was once a sinner, saved by Grace. (2) Being saved from sin. I am a joint-heir through Jesus the Christ. Apostle Paul says, "You must consider yourselves dead to sin and alive to God in Christ Jesus. For sin will have no dominion over you" (Rom. 6:11, 14 KJV). "To be dead to the ruling power of sin means that we as Christians, by virtue of the power of the Holy Spirit and the resurrection life of Christ working within us, have power to overcome the temptations and enticements of sin. Sin will no longer be our master, as once it was before we became Christians" (Grudem, 1994). We will never be able to say, "I am completely free from sin," because our sanctification will never be completed. Sanctification will be completed at death, (or our Souls) "when we get our glorified body" (Phil. 3:21 KJV), when the "Lord Returns or the 2nd Coming of Christ" (2 Cor. 3:18 KJV). I can only pray for the desire of man, to come to know and understand who God desire us to be.

I am not replying with an answer for you, but a view on this matter, to take into consideration: According to 1 Timothy 3:16 KJV, "and without controversy great is the mystery of godliness:

God was manifest in the flesh, justified in the Spirit, seen of angels, preach unto the Gentiles, believed on in the world, received up into glory" (KJV). The operative word is "mystery"; some things are just a mystery. For instance, how God blessed my mother to witness the baptizing of my father after laboring and waiting eighty-seven years, on the promise of God. Then, she went home to glory less than a year following the baptism.

Personally, I believe this is where a serious measure of faith and trust comes in with the Creator and the creation. I imagine in my little mind the "trees" have till yet to ask God, why should the leaves tremble, when the wind blows, the "waters" have till yet to ask God, why should I push "waves," when the wind blows; even the winds have till yet to ask God, why should we reply to your command, when you say to whisper from the North, South, East or West? Only mankind (the highest of his creation) will question and debate God with their actions. Here's what Matthew had to say;

Matthew 13:11-13 KJV "He answered and said unto them, because it is given to the believer to have knowledge of the mysteries of the kingdom of heaven, but to the nonbeliever it is not given. For whosoever hath, to him shall be given, and he shall have numerous overflow; but whosoever have not, from him shall be taken away even that he hath. Therefore, speak I to them in parables; because they have eyes but see not; and ears but hear not, in addition to they can't comprehend."

Basically, "God does what he pleases in the heavens and in the earth . . ." (Ps. 135:6 KJV). At times some of us will never understand or be able to simplify what or why God does what He does. Not even me! Even Moses asked God when the Israelites were in the process of "sanctification" and had fallen to worshipping idols. Moses asked, God "blot me out of the book of life," because Moses wanted the Israelite's spared, in my opinion.

- The Book of Judgement (Life/Death) (Rev. 3:5 KJV)
- The Book of Life (Exod. 32:32 KJV)
- The Book of the living (Ps. KJV)

"Our works will be written and open in the book of life, great or small, good or bad and we will be judge accordingly" (Rev. 20:12-15 KJV). "The Lord is coming swiftly, and will reward instantly, and will give to every person according to the work they have done, Good and/or Bad Deeds" (Rev. 22:12-14 KJV). "God will judge each and every one of us according to His works; we must continue to do good works. For there is no respect of person" (Rom. 2:6-11 KJV). "Wherefore, my beloved, as ye have always shown obedience, not only when I am looking, but even more that I am not looking for I am no longer here, work out your own salvation unto the Lord with fear and trembling" (Phil. 2:12 KJV). "For God will bring every act to judgment, all things that you think is hidden, be it good or evil" (Eccl. 12:14).

I believe either way it takes faith to believe or not to believe. But the Theist/Christian "walk is by 'faith' and not by sight" (2 Cor. 5:7 KJV, *The Book of Eli*). The Holy Bible was divinely inspired by forty men, "God breathed upon the men to write" (2 Tim. 3:16 KJV). Isn't it something? God breathed upon Adam in the Garden of Eden and from dust Adam became a living soul. Isn't it amazing? What God did once, He can do again! Here's an attribute of God: He's unchangeable. Therefore, He's faithful to do just what He said.

This brings this to mind for me that there are scriptures, the *logos* word or the living word, there are archaeologists who have studied through the excavation of sites and the observation and analysis of human remains, prehistorical, historical artifacts and other physical evidence, all working towards what was recorded in and of the biblical writings. Even today, archaeologists and others are still seeking "truth." What truth? This "truth" in the book of John, Jesus said, "I am the way, the truth and the life" (14:6 KJV).

Do you know there are nonbelievers that will say things like, "If this was so, someone wrote the Bible because of what they wanted others to believe." I say, they have a serious imagination. It's so serious, it's divine! I like this part even though God said, "Let us make" taking in consideration that "us" is inclusive to Jesus and the Holy Spirit. Now, we have Jesus praying for others, yet He didn't make it "all" about Him. I know because it's written in the holy Scriptures, Jesus said, "By your faith you've been made whole or by your faith you're healed."

It's strange how, when others take on the position of a "deity," it's always "all," which means *omni*, about that being. I like Jesus's version on "faith": it's unselfish; it's as if He's saying, "We're in this together." Other attributes of God are He's compassionate, personal, and about relationship and fellowship, which leads to worship.

There are many characteristics of God. Let's first begin with the attribute of God being a Sovereign Creator, or Omnipotent, meaning all-powerful. "God's exercise of power over His creation is also called God's sovereignty. God is able to do all His holy will, He doesn't need our help. Omnipotence is derived from two Latin words, 'all,' and *potens*, 'powerful,' and means 'all-power" (Grudem, 1994). God can do and will do what He decides to do, when He decides to do it. According to biblical writings, God is "The Lord, strong and mighty, the Lord, mighty in battle" (Ps. 24:8)! Many have asked, "Is there anything too hard for God?" The answer is given in the book of Jeremiah: "Nothing is too hard for God" (Jer. 32:17 KJV). God is called the "Almighty," a word that means He holds all power and authority. The angel Gabriel shares with Mary, "With God nothing will be impossible" (Luke 1:37 KJV), and Jesus puts it this way: "With God all things are possible" (Matt. 19:26 KJV). God is not limited to what He wants to do or has done. God does "whatever He pleases" (KJV). "God has shared some of His power with us, not 'all-power' but, this power is to be utilized in ways pleasing to Him and consistent with His will, which brings Him glory and reflects His own character" (Grudem, 1994).

Secondly, God is all-knowing or omniscient, which is defined as "the doctrine that God fully know and all things actual and possible in one simple and eternal act" (Grudem, 1994). John wrote, "God knows everything" (1 John 3:20 KJV).

The quality of knowing everything is called omniscience, and because of that fact, God knows all. He is said to be omniscient, which is "all-knowing." "God knows the future" (Isa. 46:9–10 KJV). Jesus said, "Your Father knows what you need prior to you asking Him" (Matt. 6:8 KJV). God knows "the strain of hair on your head are all numbered" (Matt. 10:30 KJV). "He knows our actions, words before it's on our tongue and thoughts" (Ps. 139:1–4 KJV). God told Jeremiah, "Before I formed you in the womb I knew you . . ." (1:5 KJV). Therefore, before your grandparents met, God knew you and prior to your parents meeting, God knew you.

Finally, God is all-present at the same time or omnipresence is "the doctrine that God does not have size or spatial dimensions and is present at every point of space with His whole being, yet God acts differently in different places. God is unlimited or infinite with respect to time, so God is unlimited with respect to space" (Grudem, 1994). The Latin prefix *omni* means "all." God is Lord of space; therefore, He cannot be limited by space, because He created it. God is present everywhere. David expressed God's omnipresence this way: "Wherever I go you will be there . . ." (Ps. 139:7–10 KJV). "There is nowhere in the entire universe, on land or sea, in heaven or in hell, where one can flee from God's presence. God cannot be held by any space, no matter how big it is . . ." (1 Kgs. 8:27 KJV).

God's characteristics are important to the Christian because it helps to understand who God is. God's characteristic reveals the analogy of the overarching storyline of the Bible and is needed to aid in the Christian convictions and understanding of the Creator. Hence, "the fear of the Lord is the beginning of knowledge, and the wisdom of God" (Josh. 4:24 KJV).

Therefore, the Christian will not be able to say he doesn't know the Creator or the attributes of Him. For example, the attributes of God are important because it is his attributes that informs the Christian of his "invisibility." So, when someone brings up the biblical fact your God is an "invisible" God, the Christian can say, my God is an "invisible" God, that's no surprise (Col. 1:15 KJV). When we learn more of Him, it brings us to a love of God. Here's proof of this: "God is to be feared, known, and loved as the sovereign Creator of the universe to whom all glory, honor, confident and praise is to be given" (Gen. 1–2 KJV). God's characteristics validate Him for who He is. Some attributes distinctly belong to God, and they are not shared with humanity. God's attributes show Him being personal. The attributes reveal what God has created, and, most importantly, His eternal nature. God's attributes play a huge part in the Christian enlightenment of God and the expectations of God. You see, God expects for humanity and all of creation to be redeemed and restored back to Him—yes, even, after the "fall." The attributes also reveal things that can be known about God from His awesome creation. God's attributes are so important they connect the creation to the Creator. We can only come to understand our Creator through the mind of Christ. It would be important to know the attributes if we want to know God truly, but not fully, to have an understanding of how the first act comes into existence. His attributes aid in the biblical record of creation, which God is understood and believe to be the Creator of all things;

they teach the nature of His creation, and give detailed focus to humanity, which is no doubt created in his image.

Who wouldn't like to know more about their "spiritual DNA"? The attributes of God are important because they reveal God's complete wisdom. The knowing of the attributes of God combines the Christian conviction. There are many doctrines but only one doctrine of Jesus Christ according to Christian worldview:

These important doctrines are focus on the gospel, or good news, of Jesus Christ; therefore, it may be helpful to understand that, within the Christian worldview, there are some nonnegotiable beliefs. For example; first-order points of doctrine include a belief in the Trinity (one God who exists in three persons: Father, Son, and Holy Spirit), the deity of Jesus Christ, and Jesus' resurrection from the dead. Therefore, without Jesus the Christ the redemption and restoration would be impossible. (Topic 6 Overview, 2017)

Genesis 3:2 KJV is where the woman said to the serpent, "We may eat the fruit of the trees of the garden; but of the fruit of the tree which is in the midst of the garden." God has said, "You shall not eat it, nor shall you touch it, lest you die" (KJV). Is she quoting Adam or is she quoting God? If she's quoting Adam, then, Adam shared the commandment with her (second-hand information), but if she's quoting God, then God had to tell both of them together, but this is where I can't and have not found proof in the scripture. There's only the evidence of God giving the command to Adam in scripture. Therefore, I've made an assumption that my view on this is that it's very possible Eve got second-hand information from Adam. Therefore, was she truly manipulated, or going after emulation? Or was she simply taken advantage of because it's very possible Satan knew she had second-hand information? After all, God asked Satan once before, "What are you doing?" Satan replied, "Running to and fro seeking whom I can devour" (Job KJV). Therefore, after he's taken advantage of her second hand information, he persuades her to look at the tree and it's at that time and space the tree became desirable to her mind, which the eye sees through the mind, then the heart. In Matthew 4, Satan tried to twist the truth with Jesus the Christ, but Jesus boldly said to him, "Man shall not live by bread along but, by every word that proceeded out of the mouth of God" (KJV).

If you look closely, you will find in that passage Satan tempts Jesus Christ three times. This passage conveys the example of Jesus Christ having the knowledge, wisdom, and truth of God.

Isn't it strange how whenever we find ourselves making bad decisions and as a result behaving in a bad way, we will find a place to hide from God, as if He can't see us in the nakedness of sin? If they felt it was right to eat from the tree, there would have been no reason for them to hide from God. I believe our desire of "free will" caused us to make the wrong choices, regardless of what Satan's tricks consist of. Once sin is committed, it brings shame, and after shame come silence. Satan is causing humanity to sin so that he can shame us, and even worse, silence us. If we are silenced, we will not testify of the goodness of the Lord, we will not praise, and we definitely will not worship. There goes our purpose.

But earlier, I said, Eve may not have had direct information from God that she needed. It reminds me of the Christians today who have forsaken the assembly of God (Heb. 10:25 KJV). We have abandoned weekly Bible class or Bible study, Sunday school, and worse, Sunday worship service (2 Tim 2:15 KJV), not to mention our secret devotions at home. Let's not talk about a prayer life or prayers back in the school, heaven forbid. What the world needs more than ever before is good old fashioned worship service, which nowadays is lacking due to direct communication and/or information connected to technology, which is one of the things wrong with the world: "me and technology." Yes, the possibility of someone considering the fact, Eve was no match for Satan. Satan is always running to and fro, seeking whom or what he can tear down or destroy. It's very much possible in my little world or mind, Eve was like many of us. She was naïve to a point—or was she truly and fully aware of the consequences of her "free will" choice? I often wonder why Satan went to her and not to Adam. Again, is it the possibility Satan knew Adam was given the command directly and not Eve? Therefore, he knew exactly what the order was from God in conversation with Adam. It matters who had the knowledge, who had the truth, who had wisdom, and who had understanding. Did Satan believe Eve was the weakest link? Did Satan believe Eve was not sure what the command from God said or even understood the command? Did she really know the actions of her "free will" choice?

As Christians we are constantly asked, why would God allow so much evil and suffering to happen if He is a loving God? First John 4:8-10 KJV says, "God is love." God is love, no matter what, because it is one of His many attributes. God has a loving nature. Also, if we remember, God is immutable; therefore if He wanted to change He couldn't. John 3:16 KJV, is known to be the heart of the Gospel: "For God so, love the world that He gave his only begotten Son that whosoever, believe in Him shall not perish but, have everlasting life." God loves so, that He placed the "whosoever" in John 3:16 KJV, prior to man accepting or making the "free will" choice to choose his Son, Jesus the Christ. This choice is of "free will" agent. Joshua 15:24 KJV says, "Choose ye this day whom you will serve." God allows so much to happen because He's still working on his people (Christian/Theist/Back-slider) making the right decision to choose Him. Yes, even after the fall, His work is still being processed the creation, the fall, redemption, and restoration of our relationship with Him. He wants to regain the Garden of Eden, which will be in the New Jerusalem.

Sometimes God allows tragedy to come into our lives to bring us close to Him. Sometimes God allows other things to happen to let us know that we need to depend on Him for protection, guidance, and provision. Most of us will not pray fervently until tragedy or devastation comes in our lives. Also, it keeps us humble. Apostle Paul said, "I sought the Lord three times, asked Him to remove this thorn from my flesh that it might depart from me? God answered and said, when you're weak that's when I am strong. My Grace is sufficient for thee: for my strength is made perfect in weakness" (2 Cor. 12:8–9 KJV). It doesn't matter what you've encountered, man meant it for bad but, God meant it for my good.

Sin entered by one man, the First Adam, in the Garden of Eden, and following the fall, death entered into the world. Through the death of the Last Adam, Jesus Christ, on the Hill called Calvary, resurrection was brought into the world. John wrote on an Isle of Patmos, Greece in the book of Revelation, "After this." After what? After Calvary "there will be no more pain, no more sorrow, and God will wipe the tears from your weeping eyes." Before we were redeemed by Christ, not only did we do sinful acts and have sinful attitudes, we were also sinners by nature. Apostle Paul said it like this: "While we were yet sinners Christ died for us" (Rom. 5:8 KJV); "we were by nature children of wrath, like the rest of mankind" (Eph. 2:3 KJV). Men angels (Gen. 6:3 KJV) sinned by willful, voluntary choice (Grudem, 1994).

This is what I've said; it's highly possible that the serpent was aware of Eve's indirect line of communication or lack thereof to God. Therefore, she would be the weakest link in his eyes, being that she received her information from Adam. Because she was not placed in the Garden of Eden along with Adam, during the time God issued Adam the command. She had not yet come into existence or appeared just yet. The serpent when in the Garden of Eden was running to and fro, and even today, the serpent is still running to and fro, seeking whom he may devour. We must enlighten, train, educate, and empower the saints of God in the Word of God.

Therefore, when we are in Spiritual warfare, we will know how to fight, and Satan can't twist God's word around, like he attempted to do to our very own Savior, Jesus the Christ, in the book of Matthew 4 KJV.

It is for us to be totally dependent upon God. Jesus depends on God and the Holy Spirit. We must remember in the process of salvation is justification, sanctification—regeneration, and then, glorification. So therefore, no one is perfect or born without sin, so we must accept Jesus the Christ. Apostle Paul said, "For we have all sinned and come short of the Glory of God" (Rom. 3:23 KJV). Sanctification is the longest of the process. "If we say that we have no sin, we deceive ourselves, and the truth is not in us" (1 John 1:8 KJV). We will be without sin when we get our glorified body; at this time we will be sinless. Therefore, the late Professor Cleveland E. Washington would say, "GOD PLANNED IT IN ETERNITY PASSED, JESUS PAID FOR IT ON A HILL CALLED CALVARY, AND THE HOLY SPIRIT SEALED IT, ON THE DAY OF PENTECOST" (Washington, 2015).

I believe a great deal of suffering that people experience and characterization of human nature is accurate. Because my definition of human nature together consists of more than one attribute or characteristic, in a combination of ways having to do with the ability to think, feel, and act, which is said to come naturally, according to our individual being. Even though God the Creator designed us, the creation, He made us in His image.

Therefore, God possesses his own will, and He thought enough of us to design within our very own nature, a "free will." Free will "with respect to God is all things that God decided to will but had no necessity to will according to His nature, with respect to man.

The ability to make willing choices that have real effects, however, "other people define this in other ways, including the ability to make choices that are not determined by God" (Grudem, 1994, glossary, pp. 1242-1243).

When God made us (Adam and Eve) in his image, He made us in His being or likeness. For instance, God has attributes and/or characteristics: there are attributes that God shares with us and some He doesn't. I believe God shares with us, in the attribute of "purpose," which includes "will and freedom." Apostle Paul wrote to the church of Ephesus, "Be imitators of God, as beloved children" (Eph. 5:1 KJV). What is our (humanity's) purpose in life? No doubt, to glorify Him! But, I believe God wanted Adam and Eve to glorify, to praise, to serve, and to worship him by their choice of "free will." I believe after God had given the instructions, commandment on what to do and not to do, the purpose which was to be

bless, fruitful, multiply, replenish the earth, dress it and keep or maintain it, have dominion over every living thing that move upon the earth, and name the animals, of every tree of the garden thou may freely eat: but now, for the thing not to do. I commanded you, not to eat from the tree of the knowledge of good and evil, thou shalt not eat of it: for in the day that thou eat thereof thou shalt surely die. (Gen. 1:26; 2:15-17 KJV).

It's amazing no matter what God gives us or how He blesses us, we will somehow find a way to do the thing He says not to do. Apostle Paul said it like this: "The thing I should do, I do not and the thing I should not do, that I do" (Rom. 7:15-25 KJV). God is "not a God who delights in wickedness" (Ps. 5:4 KJV), but one whose "soul hates him that loves violence" (Ps. 11:5 KJV). "Therefore, God does not take pleasure in sin; nevertheless, for his own purposes, and in a way that still remains largely a mystery to us, God ordained that sin would come into the world" (Grudem, 1994).

In Ephesians 1:11 (KJV), Apostle Paul said that we must never say that God Himself sinned or that He is to be blamed for sin. The Bible affirms that God "does according to His will" in the host of heaven and among the inhabitants of the earth and that no one can stay His hand or say to Him, "What are you doing?" (Dan. 4:35 KJV). God did ordain that sin would come into the world, even though, He does not delight in it. He ordained that it would come about through the voluntary choices of moral creatures. We must know that sin does not surprise God, and it is no challenge for Him. Let's not forget that before the fall of Adam and Eve, sin was present in the angelic world through the fall of Satan and his demons. When considering the human race, the first sin was of Adam and Eve in the Garden of Eden, Adam being the representation of all mankind. Sin opened the door to death, suffering, pain, sorrow, sickness, punishment, and so on. Apostle Paul wrote that, after the fall, "We have all sinned and come short of the glory of God" (Rom. 3:23 KJV). "For we are all conceived into sin by our mother, and look shaped into iniquity which is like a 'learning style' of having a sin nature" (Ps. 51:5 KJV). Our nature is made up of what we see, feel, know, think, and experience. The culture of your belief, customs, and environment can motivate your worldview and how you feel about certain things, act in situations, and make choices according to your "free will."

First, the sin of Adam and Eve was about wanting to know more than or as much as God. They were wondering about the truth, but God had already told them the truth in the garden. Basically, you will surely die if you violate what God said, "not to do." Satan twisted God's words. The audacity of us (creation) to doubt what God (Creator) said! Second, God told them "not to eat of the tree of the knowledge of good and evil because they would surely die" (Gen. 2:17 KJV). Here God is saying, what not to do and why it shouldn't be done, no trickery, just facts and the why. Here is where moral standards were set. Adam and Eve experienced the lust of the eye; what the eye sees the eye wants, in this case, the desire to become wise. They had a choice between what is right or wrong. Even though, free will is right here, God desires for us to choose Him every time. Third, God is our Creator, and we are His creation, but of course, always wanting more, even to be wise "like God" (Gen. 3:5 KJV). Apostle Paul calls it our lasciviousness (to be eager or have wanton, lust, desire, and pleasure), usurping authority, by any means necessary. In the New Testament, to imply, "He's our Lord and Savior" (Jer. 11:12 KJV). When basically, we want Him as Savior but not as Lord. You see, as Lord, He tells us what to do, not the other way around. Finally, according to Wayne Grudem, "All sin is ultimately irrational" (1994). The choices listed above were as irrational, foolish, and inconsiderate of the Creator, even more so with the characteristic of "free will." The choice Satan made when he went against God was because he wanted to exalt himself above God. The choice Adam and Eve made when they disobeyed God was they wanted to be as wise as God. It is the "fool" in the following passages that delights in all kinds of sins (Prov. 10:23 KJV). Our choices have consequences. We must know that sin does not surprise God and it is no challenged for God. Let's not forget before the fall of Adam and Eve, sin was present in the angelic world, the fall of Satan and demons.

But of course, Satan never wins. Since, the conflict in the spiritual realm with Satan, lasciviousness, wanting to be God, has left a world of peace disrupted by confusion and the utilization of wicked devices. Satan followed his very own act of disobedience while, in the Garden of Eden, he persuaded the creation (Eve to persuade Adam to go against the Creator), which was an overarching act of disobedience as an end result of "free will" choice. Remember Adam and Eve opened the door to Satan and the sin of evil, and sin opened the door to surely death, suffering, violence, murder, and destruction, just to name a few.

The question might come to mind, if God gave me "free will" why can't I make my own choices? This is why: not all choices are not good choices. Only the Spirit of God's wisdom, knowledge, and understanding can help you make your "will" God's will. It's called the creation; it is dependent upon the Creator and not the Creator dependent upon the creation.

Even though, there's the Creator and His creation, and—yes, Satan as the evil one. Satan is fighting the Creator for something that is not his and the "throne of God" will never be his. God Himself said, "Heaven is my Throne, and the Earth is my footstool" (Isa. 66:1 KJV). By fighting God, Satan is utilizing God's pinnacle creation, mankind. I believe, Satan believe this is somehow God's heart in an anthropomorphic way. Now, I know God is a spirit. Therefore, a Spirit has no body parts. But, Satan is desperate to bring God down. You know, some things will never change. Satan was up in heaven fighting, and until this day, he's still here on Earth fighting, going against God, and gathering mankind to go against God. Therefore, it's late in the day; he's trying all he has. God told us (mankind) from his Word (the Bible) to "love ye one another: As I have loved you" (John 13:34 KJV). Satan persuades us not to do that by causing confusion between the following: spouses, parents and children, siblings among siblings, supervisors and subordinates, neighbors, and worst, even in the church family of pastor and flock, sister and brothers in Christ. Then, God steps in after Satan works his evil and wicked devices like the attack on 9/11, Coronavirus of 2020, natural disasters like the tsunami of 2004, and God lets mankind know that "I am still God, and I am still the Supreme Maker and Ruler of Heaven and Earth" and I am here to walk with you through it all. I'll give you a way of escape (1 Cor. 10:13 KJV).

Why? Because God takes what Satan meant for bad and turns it to good. God is not the author of confusion and/or evil. God is "not a God who delights in wickedness" (Ps. 5:4 KJV) but one whose "soul hates him that loves violence" (Ps. 11:5 KJV); therefore, "God does not take pleasure in sin; nevertheless, for His own purposes, and in a way that still remains largely a mystery to us, God ordained that sin would come into the world" (Grudem, 1994).

Every time the creation goes against the Creator's plan, it will cause disturbance in the world, the White House/country, the family house/home, the relationship/marriage, the children, the house of prayer/church house, the school house, the elderly house/living center, and yes the jail house too. I like the way the late evangelist William Franklin Graham, Jr. said:

Act of violence in references to 9/11 affirmed our conviction that God cares for us, even after 9/11, no matter what ethnic, religious or political background may be. The Bible says that "He is the God of all comfort, who comforts us in all our troubles." It doesn't matter the horror, the shock and the revulsion we all feel over what took place in this nation on Tuesday morning (Graham, 2001).

Jeremiah declares firmly, "The heart is more deceitful above all things and is desperately sick, who can understand it?" (17:9 KJV). The heart itself is an obstacle to overcome and an enemy to be defeated and then, there is Satan.

Now, here's another question. Is evil real? It is when tragedy comes The Bible is no longer writing to us on what to do, but it is now causing us to act upon what we should do or need to do by way of example. For instance, "love you one another or be kind ye one to another" during days like 9/11 yes, we are kind to one another, helping one another, strangers and all. If it was any other day, would we be kind to one another? Therefore, disasters like the tsunami of 2004 and the attack on 9/11 is meant for bad, but God works in the aftermath for the good.

Apostle Paul told the Romans, "So we know that all things work together for good to those who love God, to those who are the called according to His purpose" (KJV). This is the way to handle our problems:, give it to God and STOP worrying about it. After, we give it to Him. Thank Him on what He's about to do! Yes, thank Him for the good and bad! God will no doubt see you through the good, bad, and the ugly. But that knowledge doesn't give me the right to utilize God's grace as an excuse to do what I want, as in making bad choices. I consult God even more now, prior to my "will or way." Even if I have no choice, I continue to thank Him. It's not easy, but it's out of love, respect, and trust for the God I serve and have come to love, respect, and truly but not fully understand.

Chapter 4

● ● ● ● ●

Saved to Live out My Purpose

It was August 29, 2005, while serving in the armed forces (USAF), I was ordered to return to New Orleans, two days during the aftermath of a catastrophic natural disaster. It was then, besides the death of a loved one, that my faith was tested. It was then, that my world view as a theist became so real. I grew in faith through leaps and bounds. I didn't know that level of devastation until a catastrophic natural disaster named Hurricane Katrina embraced me with her presence by entering the Gulf of Mexico, Plaquemines Parish, and then the city of New Orleans. I knew how to cry out to God for myself, but not yet for others. I was ordered to convoy back to New Orleans accompanied by an element of a twelve-person team, including a Chaplin named Lt. Col. Timothy Neustifter. The convoy seemed as if we were riding forever, like we weren't going to arrive. No one was talking; as I looked around the younger airmen were asleep, and you could see the anxiety in the eyes of those who were awake, yet committed with passion to the call, but when I looked over at the chaplain, he was doing what a chaplain does. I watched him as he watched over all of us, and I couldn't go to sleep. I didn't totally understand his duty, but eventually I did. The chaplain and I became spiritually connected, and I thank him for being there

Why did God save Me?

when I needed it the most, not knowing what we were going to encounter upon the entrance to the city. We were riding in a duce and a half, departing a military unit located in Northern Louisiana traveling down south of Louisiana, towards Orleans and Plaquemines. I remembered upon the entrance to the town of La Place and then, the city of New Orleans; you can see, feel, and smell the intense rumor of death—it was distinct. As far as the eye could see, the grass was no longer green, the water had a sour sense of smell, and there was no movement of life except the military convoy traveling on the only highway that was open to the entrance of the parish at the time. I saw one hundred-plus year-old trees had been ripped out the ground and paths of physical destruction like tornado alley with tornados on a scale of EF-5, or an earthquake on a scale of 8.0. I remembered asking God, as the tears swelled up in my eyes but yet not streaming down my face. Why are you so angry? What have we done to cause you to be so angry? "It's a fearful thing to full into the hands of an angry God" (Heb. 10:31 KJV). God answered me with the words from the book of Jeremiah 23:1–40 and Ezekiel 34 chapter, 11 through 31, KJV "I myself will be their Shepherd. I will search for my sheep and take care of them." I believed, in this season, we as God's people had stopped taking care of one another, looking out for each other, loving each other. Even pastors (spiritual leaders) had turned away from God. Of course, it reminded me of the fall, selfish desires. Everyone was for themselves, and no one was looking out for the babies, the elderly, and the fools. This is a glimpse of things I've encountered through this particular tragedy.

There were many who were left behind during Hurricane Katrina by their pastors, and if not the pastor the church. The scriptures mentioned above validate what really happened to the churches and/or the flock. The prophet Jeremiah wrote, "Woe is unto the pastors that destroy and scatter the sheep of my pasture! Said the Lord" (23:1 KJV).

While serving in the 159th Fighter Wing, I had a commander walk up to me and begin to share with me about his pastor. This pastor had a congregation the size of about 7,000-plus. The commander shared with me following: during Katrina his pastor quit the pastoral care office. I asked, the commander, did the pastor quit or did God fire him? The commander wanted to know what I meant. I asked, was he familiar with the scriptures about Jeremiah 23 and Ezekiel 34, how God gave warnings to the pastors about the flock, his sheep, being scattered.

When we spend time in the word, we come to know the truth. Jesus said, "I am the way, the truth, and the life" (John 14:6 KJV). To know the truth, is to know God. Truth is validated by the word of God. When spending time in the word and studying the word, we will know when it's God speaking to us, and we will understand what God is saying to us. Paul refers to "scripture as the word of truth" (2 Tim. 2:15 KJV). After the acceptance of God the Son, you can begin to communicate with God the Father and God the Holy Spirit through the word of God. God is revealed through His word. God's nature and will is revealed through the word of God. The person of Jesus Christ is revealed through the word of God. Upon the approach to truth both Plato and Aristotle agree, "Truth is an accurate description of reality" (Jibben, 2015, chapter 7).

Yes, as pastor, theologian, and author Rick Warren would say:

> You can't begin your life's purpose by focusing on yourself. The creation must begin with the Creator. Your existence is God's will, he spoke you into being. You exist only because it's God's will that you exist. You were made by God and for God, and until you understand that, life will

never make sense. It is only in God that we engage, embrace, and find our origin, our identity, our meaning, our purpose, our significance, and our destiny. All paths lead to a dead end, except the path given by God. (Warren, 2002, p.17)

"Missio Dei... God Himself is a self-sending God, a missionary God, who does not wait for people to come to Him or for the world to be restored. Instead, God actively goes to the world and to individuals, because that is who He is by nature. The theological point that mission is an attribute of God is called *missio Dei. Missio Dei,* which means 'mission of God' or 'sending of God' is rooted in an understanding of the essential nature of the Trinity that results in the action of mission. God sent Himself to the world through Jesus Christ. God the Father and God the Son sent the Holy Spirit. God the Father, God the Son, and God the Holy Spirit send the church into

the world, empowered by the Holy Spirit to carry forth God's mission of salvation and healing to the broken world" (Bosch, 1991, as cited in Laing, 2009; Bosch, 1991, as cited by Guder, 2005). The theology of *missio Dei* has implications for Christ followers and the church today.

Frederick Buechner, author, pastor, and theologian, said,

A good way to find your purpose, to know what mission God is calling you to, is to discern the work "that you most need to do and that the world most needs to have done" (Buechner, 2013, para. 4). He went on to say, that if you enjoy your work, but it is meaningless, then you have probably not found your purpose. If you are doing work that is meaningful for the world but you are miserable doing it you have not found your purpose either. He sums up the idea by saying, "The place where God calls you to be the place where your deep gladness and the world's deep hunger meet." (Buechner, 2013, para. 5)

"One may find their purpose through "spending time with God it will teach you to love God" (Topic 7 overview, 2017), or as Buechner would say, "where your need meet the needs of others" (Buechner, 2013, para. 5). One might ask, "How do you spend time with God?" Study the word of God, and allow the Holy Spirit to help you understand how God communicate through the Holy Spirit to humanity. Having a purpose in life is learning "to pray to God, in the name of Jesus." When God created humanity He also designed us with a purpose. It's the divine will of God. For instance, the "eye has a purpose, the ear has a purpose and so on, every part of our being have a purpose" (1 Cor. 12:12–27 KJV), no doubt we do too. Therefore, accept the fact that God designed humanity in a unique way. Our physical DNA is designed solely to each individual. Let's look a little closer. God designed us so uniquely that each individual has his or her own finger- and footprints, which identify each individual. Even identical twins have different finger- and footprints. We are so uniquely designed by the love of God. It seems as though, prior to accepting Jesus Christ we are wandering about in the world, as a nonbeliever born into sin. After accepting Jesus Christ we are wandering even more, thirsting after the "living word," the way the Samaritan woman thirsted for the "living water" (John

4:4-42 NIV), and when Christ thirsted on the cross for our souls. God the Father, the Son, and the Holy Spirit gave us gifts for the edifying of the church, and those gifts are "our contribution to the mission" (Topic 7 overview, 2017). The spiritual gifts and the fruits of the Spirit are placed in us by the Trinity. These are what make up our character, and our character make up who we are in Christ. Your purpose will be incubated by your passion. In other words, if and when you find what you love then, you will find your purpose. If what you are doing does not "bring Glory to God" (Topic 7 overview, 2017), it's definitely a sign most likely that's not your purpose or mission because when you're walking in your purpose and working to complete your mission, God will be pleased and so will you. It is written in the scripture the order of our life, purpose, and mission will transform when we come to learn and obey the will of God, to love the Lord thy God with all thy heart, mind, and soul and "to love ye one another" (Topic 7 overview, 2017). The rest (purpose and mission) will be command by God to fall in place. According to the book of Matthew "the call to go and make disciples was not restricted to the people gathered on a hillside in Galilee that day. That call is for all people at all times in all places that follow Jesus" (Matt. 28:19-20 KJV). God's plan is demonstrated throughout the New Testament that his "followers would come together in communities to worship, to pray, to share in the Lord's table, and to care for one another" (Acts 2:42 KJV).

I've answered to the call as a follower of Christ. I've found my purpose, I am at peace with what I do, I love what I do, it brings me joy, and I know God is pleased. I am in the beginning process of my purpose; I still I have not yet arrived. I've answered the call as the elect lady of God to do "pastoral care for the last seven years" (Rom. 8:28 KJV). I've served my country, but nothing has brought me love, joy, peace, and fulfillment like the sharing and spreading of the Gospel of Jesus Christ.

Chapter 5

● ● ● ● ●

Saved for Eternity

Prior to one becoming a Christian after accepting Jesus the Christ as his Lord and Savior, then reciting the following scripture(s) in the presence of believers as witnesses, "If I confess with my mouth Jesus is Lord, and believe in my heart that God has raised His Son Jesus the Christ from the dead, then thy will be saved" (Rom. 10:9–10 KJV). "We know that we have passed from death to life, because we love each other. Anyone who does not love remains in death" (1 John 4:13 KJV). After the convert confesses his/her faith, then, the candidate will be submerged in the liquid grave, to show the world he's on the Lord's side. However, the baptism is symbolic for what's on the inside working on the outside (the Holy Spirit) of one's heart, and it's expressed to the world. Oh what a change in the believer's life. The process of salvation is as follows: "Salvation is a onetime instant legal act" (Grudem, 1994, Glossary). Justification is what Jesus did on a hill called Calvary with his blood. Sanctification is the quality of holiness or being made or becoming holy, which is the longest part of the process. Finally, glorification is the last stage of all the above. It refers to the believer after death and judgment. The highlight of it all is "redemption" (Rom. 8:29–30 KJV).

It's also written in Matthew 5:16, "To let your light so shine before men, that they may see your good works, and glorify your

Father which is in heaven" (KJV). Think about it when you're at home: your spouse, children, and siblings are all watching you, especially if they don't read the Bible. You'll reflect it to them as a living stone that can silently proclaim the living word. This is done by living your life according to the word of God. If you're on your job, at the school, in the neighborhood they are watching too. Don't limit the proclamation of the word of God to the pulpit on Sunday mornings. I personally call that indirectly, "Great Mission Work," which is also part of God's plan that He has for you. One might ask, "Why can't I teach and preach the Word of God and live however, I want to?" You've heard preachers say, do as I say, not as I do. Well, you need to be praying about whether you remain as a member at that local church or continue under that doctrine or teaching because the message of the Gospel of Jesus Christ is more effective when one not only teaches and preaches the doctrine of Jesus Christ but lives according to the doctrines and teachings of Jesus Christ. For example, to teach and preach is for those that can hear but, what about those that can't hear yet can still see. God's word is all inclusive, and we want the Gospel of Jesus Christ to reach all by hearing and by sight. Therefore, "guard your character and conduct in the word of God so you remain qualified to serve" (Luke 14:34–35 KJV).

According to the book of Genesis 3:15, the proto is *evangelion* or *evangelium*, which means the first gospel. It is written, after the fall of Adam and Eve, in the Garden of Eden that God gave us victory to overcome evil. Yes, victims overcome to be victors. Therefore, even though we were to experience sorrow, sufferings, pain, and death, He also, ensured us we will through it all have the victory over Satan. I am hoping that my sharing in my testimonies will help you, as well as others. Why else would we share in the wisdom, knowledge, understanding, and experience of God?

Saved For Eternity

Apostle Paul wrote to the church of Philippi, "That I may know Him, and the power of His resurrection, and the fellowship of His sufferings, being made conformable unto His death" (KJV). If, we truly come to know what the end will be, this is victory. Then, we can focus on that as we go through life. Then, not only have God tolerated our sinful ways but definitely found "a way of escape for us" (1 Cor. 10:13 KJV). The opportunity for evil to exist among us is a mystery, yet God told us it would be present by the voluntary choices of moral creatures.

Just a couple of months ago, we as Americans were fighting one another; we were swiftly going backwards some 300-plus years. Lo and behold!

In an anthropomorphic way the hand of God began to move upon the earth just as He said, in second Chronicles 7:12-14 and also in Isiah 26:20-21.

Here are three types of shutdown, and if you live long enough, you will witness all three. A regular shutdown is when the US government shuts down, which occurs when there is a failure to pass funding legislation to finance the government for its next fiscal year. Secondly, a premium shutdown is when the land becomes plagued with pestilence and locusts like the Coronavirus (COVID-19), which has and will affect the shutdown of the economy if the Centers for Disease Control and Prevention (CDC) doesn't control the spread of the virus. Third, the ultimate supreme shutdown is when heaven shuts down as it is written in 2 Chronicles 7:12-14 KJV, whether you know it or not the two are governed by the latter. Believe me, God does as He pleases. This country need to get back to "thus says the Lord." After all we say we're one nation under God. Oh, and why do we say God bless America when America is no longer blessing God?

A couple of days prior to March 12, 2020 here in the United States (US) I stood in front of the TV watching CNN report what was going on in Italy. During the beginning stage of the pandemic here in the US it was easy to observe as people were moving about, the anxiety and fear in their faces was obvious, not necessarily hearing their voices because no one was talking, which is abnormal for Southerners, only because it's "that look" when passing each other in the grocery stores in the aisle where the shelves were empty or at the gas station as you filled your vehicle with gas. The people were stocking up on food, water, tissue paper, paper towels, and cleaning products. The grocery stores were running out of the items listed above. As New Orleanais, we know how to deal with hurricane preparedness but where are the virus preparedness guidelines? It was reported that in Italy the crematory was working twenty-four hours a day, and they were still behind. The Catholic Church had coffin, after coffin, after coffin. I now know and understand that Death is an accurate description of reality. In Madrid, Spain, it was reported 2,696 dead bodies were being stored on an ice ring (Palacio De Hielo). The hospital beds, the church funerals, and the graveyards were all full.

On March 12, 2020, about 10:00 a.m., I was watching a live News Break on Fox Channel 8, the US Surgeon General Vice Admiral Jerome Adams, MD, Governor John Bel Edwards, and Mayor Latoya Cantrell were reporting to the American people how we must come together and look out for one another. Well, what's ironic about that is this is exactly what Jesus Christ told us to do some 2,000 years ago. I was more astonished, at the words I heard than watching the leaders stand in front of the podium. For every word they said, I heard the voice of God. For instance, Adams said, "preparing is not panicking, panic and fear is not good, get the facts from coronavirus.gov it will help you put things into context. Do not travel to hotspots, or gather in crowds over 250, a couple of days later that number decline to 10 folks or less and stay as far as 6 feet apart from one another, the novel coronavirus-COVID-19 is critical towards chronic illness and seniors with chronic illnesses, so far these are the symptoms; coughs, shortness of breath, and fever. There are some patients who will recover and there are some who will not recover from this virus. Remember to look out for one another."

The governor said, "I believe in prayer! We must pray and take care of each other." The mayor said, the same: "Look out for each other." I am just saying, we all should be ashamed of ourselves. It takes a catastrophic disaster to bring us back to ground zero, our faith.

Let's wake up, people! It takes all of this for us to "be ye kind one to another" (Eph. 4:32 KJV). Did you hear and see God mentioned above? Is this the only way for the people of God to come together and pray?

It takes COVID-19 to stop the world from turning, it stopped trains on its tracks, it stopped planes from flying in the air, it stopped travelers from traveling, and stopped ships out at sea. Those that were employed immediately became unemployed; it was reported within a week, about 3.3 million people had applied for unemployment and at this time there were other states unaware of the rapid growth with unemployment, not knowing it was just a couple more days, and the high unemployment rate would be in each state of the US along with the COVID-19 virus. Almost 99 percent of the businesses in the Epicenter doors were closed. The COVID-19 virus was not visible but somehow made its presence known. When the government ordered the National Quanta tine "we the people" didn't understand that this would take the eyes, hands, and the feet away from the virus, it had no means of travel. There were people gathering in crowds on the beach of Florida and California (CNN, 2020). But, humanity is so strong-minded when it comes to the gift of free will. Somehow our first choice is most likely driven by our lasciviousness. The result of our actions gives evidence of where you're located spiritually and not geographically. After Adam had sinned against

God, God asked, "Adam, where are thou?" (Gen. 3:9 KJV). It wasn't a geographic question; it was a spiritual one because God knew exactly where he placed Adam, but God was asking Adam about his heart. What have you done! Whenever there's a choice to be made and your first choice is, what would I do?, this is definitely a sign. However, if you say what would Jesus do?, it is then, you've begin growing and moving spiritually in the right direction. Now, you're on your way walking by "first-faith" and not by sight (2 Cor. 5:7 KJV).

We're still not praying as one nation under God. Still there are no prayers in the schools. I am wondering why today everyone is banned from the school. Schools are closed for the COVID-19 virus. Still there are no prayers together in the local church. I am wondering why this is. Everyone is banned from the local churches. Still there are no prayers and visitation in the living centers. I am wondering why today everyone is banned from visiting the living centers? Still there are no prayers and visitation in the jailhouse and prisons. I am wondering why the jailhouse and prisons are being limited to who all visit? Look and listen a little closer at what's really going on! If God is not talking, I don't know who is.

If you really know he's talking, do you know what he's saying? "If my people, who are called by my name, shall humble themselves, and pray, and seek my face, turn from their wicked ways; then will you hear from heaven, and will forgive their sin, and will heal their land" (2 Chr. 7:14 KJV). We need to put faith first. How? By putting God first. Such as, reconsider the following; (1) the White House country must reconsider praying as one nation under God. (2) The family house must reconsider secret devotions. (3) The school house must reconsider our children praying together. (4) The elderly house must reconsider prayer and visitation for them. (5) The jail house must reconsider prayer and visitation for them. (6) The hospital house must reconsider prayer for the people and better health care. (7) Numerous employers must reconsider allowing the employees who are people of faith to not work on Sundays. Did we leave God out? Most definitely!

Again, is evil real? It is when tragedy comes. The Bible is no longer writing to us on what to do, but it is now causing us to act upon what we should do or need to do by way of example. For instance, "love ye one another or be kind ye one to another" during days like 9/11—yes, we were kind to one another, helping one another, strangers and all. If, it was any other day, would we be kind to one another? Therefore, disasters like the Tsunami of 2004 and the attack on 9/11, Hurricane Katrina, and COVID-19 virus are meant for bad, but God works in the aftermath for the good. When we were hit with the COVID-19 virus, it was reported by CNN and Johns Hopkins University and Medicine, as of March 20, 2020, there were 246,444 confirmed cases, 10,040 deaths, 86,036 recovered in the world. In the USA, there were 14,250 confirmed cases, 205 deaths, and 121 recovered. In the UK it was reported 2,716 confirmed cases, 138 deaths, and 67 recovered. After watching the Coronavirus Pandemic in Wuhan, China, Northern Italy, and Madrid, Spain, the people in the US began to panic, the virus that we thought was over there, is now over here as the number of cases continued to rise, globally. The American norm was no more in the land, the land that once believed in one nation under God. It seem as though America in such a times as this appear to be questioning its beautiful, as many lie in the hospital beds dying, all alone without their loved ones, and the family left with no closure. Believe me when I say, I know the level of degrees of pain you feel. There was a nurse on the front line who said, "There's no medical supplies, no mask, no ventilators, and no protective gear," and then she added, in a tone of disappointment and despair, "I thought this was a first-world country, this is unacceptable." In other words, what happened to America, the leading country, or America, the beautiful (CNN,2020). As of April 1, 2020, it was reported Coronavirus Pandemic globally had total cases of 1,721, 353 and deaths; there were 104,800 in the US, and total cases of 501,701 with deaths at 18,781 (CNN, John Hopkins University, 2020). In the state of Louisiana, the Fox 8 local news channel reported 537 confirmed cases and 14 deaths, and the numbers are expected to rise exponentially. As of April 11, 2020, the numbers had increase to 18,283 confirmed cases and 702deaths. At this time the spread had not reached its peak. It's also said, this can go on, with an early projection date of May and the late projection date of August. People are dying, and if you're not lying in a hospital bed sick with COVID-19 virus you're among the 3.3 million who applied for unemployment within a week while waiting on another enemy called starvation.

Well, I believe everybody have a right to "dream" but, to hear Donald Trump say on national TV/CNN, "The people want to go back to work, they need to go back to work. We the people will fill the church house on Easter Sunday morning, it will be great!"

How can you go back to work when the medical subject matter experts says, the spread of the virus have not reached its peak. On March 28, Dr. Anthony Fauci, Director of National Institute of Allergy and Infectious Disease said, "The virus is the boss; the virus makes the timeline" (CNN, 2020). Meanwhile, the epidemiology department was researching and experimenting for immunization, vaccine, and/or even a cure, but it proved true; the virus was appearing to be the boss.

Evidently, the premium shutdown closed many doors—the door to the White House, governor's house, mayor's house (office), church house, schoolhouse, jail house, and—my God—the house for seniors.

Time was of the essence and this plague was no ally to the United States; it was definitely a medical war zone, just without guns and knives. Our greatest weapon was to revert back to what

God told us from the beginning, love ye one another and be our brother's keeper. The Federal and Local Government said, save lives by staying home. The attack from COVID-19 was heinous. It was as if it had a mind of its own, it was strengthening, and increase speed by spreading.

I didn't know Andrew Cuomo, the Governor of New York, until recently. I've come to know him by watching him on CNN. He showed a serious amount of compassion for the people of God, or as he would say, compassion for New Yorkers. I loved it when he said, "I work for each and every one of you" (CNN, 2020). He went on to say, "You think the first respondents are not afraid to go to work, day after day, sure they're afraid but, they've found something greater than fear it's called passion" (CNN, 2020). It reminded me of one of my favorite quotes by Dr. Martin Luther King, Jr.: "If a man hasn't found something he will die for, he isn't fit to live" (King, 2015).

Life after death: this is what the Christians are saved for—to spend eternity with God. In days like these, the question is not are you prepared to live but, are you prepared to die? Where will you spend eternity? We've been so busy planning to live, no one planned to die!

We were saved to be a beacon of light to others, to take an account prior to departing this place. If you had to depart this very day and very hour, ask yourselves this question. How many did you guide, instruct, and lead home, not to their physical home of record but to their spiritual home called heaven bound.

Remember, remember, and remember, "It all starts with God. He's not just the starting point of your life; He is the source of it" (Warren, 2002, p.20). To find your purpose only God can assist you, no matter how many people are in our lives or entering our lives. Your life is so precious it must be structured on eternal truth.

Remember according to John, Jesus said, "I am the way, the truth, and the life" (14:6 KJV). Now, when reading and studying the Bible or the word of God, we not only have the way and truth, but we have the life, too. As we read and study the word of God, He begins to reveal Himself to us—remember "special revelation" (Pasley, 2015, chapter 11)? Now, we can look at God from a different perspective, not with the eyes of the flesh but with spiritual eyes, because He's a personal and spiritual God. Now, I pray you focus on God's mission, who will guide you in focusing on humanity's mission, which of course, involves your purpose. "You discover your identity and purpose through a relationship with Jesus Christ. It's not about you or me" (Warren, 2002, p.20).

In chapter one I'd spoken about God and suffering. Well, nothing has changed; God can't change part of His character. However, suffering can change, and it will. Suffering ends at the beginning of one's eternal life.

The more Satan stays focused on you, you stay focus on Jesus. Let's stay focused on the positive (Jesus) not the negative (Satan).

About the Author

Dr. Simone Michele Duplessis, ThD, is an African American woman who has founded and pastors a nondenominational church in the twenty-first century (2013), where she has taken in a total of 243 souls and is now serving the people of God in the State of Louisiana. She is also retired as a disabled veteran of the United States Air Force and the Louisiana Air National Guard of twenty years (2014). She has one son she is very proud of, her beloved son, James T. Bridges, Jr.

As of this year she's a newly appointed Professor of Boutte Community Bible College (2020). Her education consists of an associate in occupational studies in business; an administration degree from Philip Junior College of Gulfport, Mississippi, and Louisiana (1985) graduating with honors (President's List); associate in applied science education and training; a management degree from the Community College of the Air Force (2009); a bachelor of Christian education degree from Union Baptist College and Theological Seminary(1999); a master of theology from Union Baptist College and Theological Seminary (2017); a doctorate in theology degree from Slidell Baptist Seminary (2019), graduating with honors (Cum Laude); and currently is working on a psychology degree at Grand Canyon University (2019). She's certified as a congregational health promoter and wellness ministry leader by Congregational Wellness Baptist Community Ministries (2020).

Her purpose in life is to glorify God, and her role as a pastor is to serve the people of God. She was licensed by Holy Trinity Christian Baptist Church (2002) of New Orleans and ordained by the Ecclesiastical Conclave of Violet, Louisiana, on November 10, 2006.

She's the founding pastor of Ecclesia of Christ Fellowship Center in Gretna, future home at 3737 Wall Blvd., New Orleans, Louisiana.

Since her early childhood she's been diligently seeking God. She currently resides on the West Side of New Orleans area.

She loves to enlighten, educate, and train and empower the people of God in the Word of God, in the church from the pulpit to the pews on Sunday morning, preaching the word, to Wednesday afternoon, going out to the Naval Air Station—Joint Reserve Base, teaching base Bible class to the men and women serving in the armed forces, and to the Thursday nights Bible class at EOC.

Bibliography

Bowen, William (2016). *"Hurt people hurt people,"* http://www.WillBowen.com

Diffey, 2015. *The Beginning of Wisdom:* "An Introduction to Christian Thought and Life," e-book, chapter 3" "The Topic Overview 1 and Chapter 2 in *The Beginning of Wisdom: An Introduction to Christian Thought and Life.*" Retrieved from http://gcumedia.com/digital-resources/grand-canyon-university/2015/the-beginning-of-wisdom_an-introduction-to-christian-thought-and-life_ebook_2e.php

Graham, W. (2001). http://www.billygrham.org/story/a-day-to-remember-a-day-of-victory/#

Grudem, Wayne, 1994. *Systematic Theology,* chapter 11, p.173, chapter 12, p.190, chapter 13, pp. 216–217. Glossary p. 1255, pp. 746–747.

Jibben, J. *The Wisdom of Absolutes. The Beginning of Wisdom an Introduction to Christian Thought and Life,* 2016, lc.gcumedia.com/cwv101/the-beginning-of-wisdom-an-introduction-to-christian-thought-and-life/v2.1/#/chapter 7

King, M. (2015). http://www.youtube.com, goodreads.com

Kreeft, P. (2014). *God and Suffering.* Prageru Website 2014. Retrieved from https://prageru.com/video/god-and-suffering

Merriam-Webster dictionary.https://www.merriam-webster.com

Pasley, M. (2015). *Practical wisdom.* In Grand Canyon University (Ed.), *The beginning of wisdom: An introduction to Christian thought and life* (2nd ed.). Retrieved from https://lc.gcumedia.com/cwv101/the-beginning-of-wisdom-an-introduction-to-christian-thought-and-life/v2.1/#/chapter/11

Resources: CNN Live and CNN On scene, John Hopkins University and Medicine, Fox 8 local news channel, 20 March 2020, 1April 2020, 11 April 2020, *Coronavirus Pandemic,* Cooper, A., Dr. Gupta, S., Cuomo, C. and Lemon, D., Lavandera, E. *The Book of Eli,* directed by Albert & Allen Hughes, (Motion Picture, 2010), produced by Susan, J., Andrew, D., Broderick, K., Washington, J., written by Whitta, G.

The Holy Bible. *KJV.* Biblica, 2011.

Topic 6 Overview. (2017). CWV-101: *Christian Worldview.* Phoenix, AZ: Grand Canyon University.

Warren, Rick, 1954- (2002). *The Purpose Driven Life:* What on Earth Am I Here for? Grand Rapids, Mich.: Zondervan.

Washington, Cleveland E., (2015). Professor at Union Baptist College and Theological Seminary, New Orleans.

Summary

I am struggling to understand why an all knowing, all loving, and all powerful God would allow this manner of suffering to come upon his people. If you've survived one of the following moral evils that are done by humanity, and natural disasters, such as hurricane, flood, 9/11 attack, tsunami, wildfire, earthquake, tornado, blizzard, snow storm, cold or heat wave, volcano, drought, chronic illnesses, sarcoma/cancer, pestilences, plagues, and last, Coronavirus COVID-19, and wondering why God saved you, he saved you for a reason, your mission, and his purpose.

Why did it take COVID-19 to stopped the world from turning? It stopped trains in its tracks, it stopped planes from flying in the air and it stopped travelers from traveling, and stopped ships out at sea. Those that were employed immediately became unemployed. It was reported by CNN, Johns Hopkins University and Medical within a week, about 3.3 million people had applied for unemployment and at this time there were other states unaware of the rapid growth with unemployment, not knowing it was just a couple more days, and the high unemployment rate would be in each state of the US along with the COVID-19 virus. Almost 99 percent of the businesses in the Epicenter doors were closed. The COVID-19 virus was not visible but somehow made its presence known. When the government ordered the National Quanta tine "we the people" didn't understand that this would take the eyes, hands, and the feet away from the virus because it had no means of travel.

List of Scriptures:

Genesis 2–3
Jeremiah 29:13
Proverbs 22:6
Philippians 1:6
Job 1–3
Phil 3:10
Matthew 5:11–12
Genesis 37–50
Proverbs 14:12
Phil. 2:5
John 12:32
Romans 8:5–8
Romans 8:28
Romans 15:1
Genesis 1:11
Nehemiah 10:8
Genesis 50:20
Genesis 3:8
John 14:1–7
John 1:1–3
1 Corinthians 3:6
1 John 3:2
1 Corinthian 15:52
Proverbs 1:7
Exodus 3:20

Why did God save Me?

John 4:24
1 Peter 2:9
John 10:32
Galatians 5:19-21
Matthew 12:46-50
Jeremiah 1:5
Isaiah 9:6
Genesis 14:19; Psalm 146:6
Romans 8:38
Psalm 27:14
Luke 4:24
2 Corinthians 5:7
Genesis 16:7-16; Proverbs 15:3; Ecclesiastes 12:1-14
Psalm 14:1
Romans 8:2-30
Matthew 28:20
Psalm 145
Psalm 38:4
John 15:4
Titus 3:5
Romans 6:11, 14
Phil. 3:21
2 Cor. 3:18
1 Corinthians 10:13
Phil.3:13-14
Colossians 3:10
1 Peter 1:5
1 Timothy 3:16
Matthew 13:11-13
Psalm 135:6
Revelation 3:5
Exodus 32:32
Revelation 12:15

List Of Scriptures:

Romans 2:6-11
Phil 2:12
Eccl. 12:14
2 Corinthians 5:7
2 Timothy 3:16
John 14:6
Psalm 24:8
Jeremiah 32:17
Luke 1:37
Matthew 19:26
1 John 3:20
Isaiah 46:9-10
Matthew 6:8
Matthew 10:30
Psalm 139:1-4
Jeremiah 1:5
Psalm 139:7-10
1 Kings 8:27
Joshua 4:24
Col. 1:15
Genesis 1-2
Genesis 3:2
Matthew 4
Hebrews 10:25
2 Timothy 2:15
1 John 4:8-10
John 3:16
Joshua 15:24
2 Corinthians 12:8-9
Romans 5:8
Ephesians 2:3
Genesis 6:3
Romans 3:23

Why did God save Me?

1 John 1:8
Ephesians 5:1
Genesis 1:26, 2:15-17
Romans 15:25
Psalms 5:4
Psalm 11:5
Ephesians 1:11
Daniels 4:35
Romans 3:23
Psalm 51:5
Genesis 3:5
Proverbs 10:23
Isaiah 66:1
John 13:34
1 Corinthians 10:13
Psalms 5:4
Psalms 11:5
Jeremiah 17:9
Hebrews 10:31
Jeremiah 23:1-40, Ezekiel 34:11-31
Jeremiah 23 and Ezekiel 34
John 14:6
2 Timothy 2:15
1Cor. 12:12-27
John 4:4-42
Matthew 28:19-20
Acts 2:42
Romans 8:28
Romans 10:9-10
1 John 4:13
Romans 8:29-30
Matthew 5:16
Luke 14:34-35

List Of Scriptures:

Genesis 3:15
1 Corinthian 10:13
2 Chronicles 7:14
Isiah 26:20-21
2 Chronicles 7:12-14
Ephesian 4:32
2 Corinthians 5:7
Matthew 28:20
Genesis 2:17
Genesis 3:5
Jeremiah 11:12
Job

Note: All cited Scripture references were from the King James Version of the Bible.

CPSIA information can be obtained
at www.ICGtesting.com
Printed in the USA
LVHW051135060623
748990LV00002B/240